P9-ECL-947

DAVID LEATHERBERRY
with BOB ABBOTT

AFGHANISTAN,
MY TEARS

AFGHANISTAN,
MY TEARS

BY DAVID LEATHERBERRY
with BOB ABBOTT

Afghanistan, My Tears
By David Leatherberry with Bob Abbott

Second Edition

Printed in the United States of America
ISBN: 1-880689-18-9
Copyright 2007, David Leatherberry

Cover design by KeyArt
Cover photography by Ken Horn

Unless otherwise indicated, all Scripture references are from the Holy Bible: New International Version, © 1984, Zondervan Bible Publishers.

All Afghan names and most other names have been changed. Some circumstances and identities have been altered, but not in such a way as to distort the truth of the story or portrayal of the characters.

All rights reserved. No portion of this book may be used without written permission of the author, with the exception of brief excerpts for magazine articles, reviews, etc.

Additional copies of this book may be obtained by writing to Onward Books, Inc., 4848 South Landon Court, Springfield, MO 65810.

To my wife, Julie

"A wife of noble character ... is worth
far more than rubies."

Proverbs 31:10

To the people of Afghanistan

"Streams of tears flow from my eyes
because my people are destroyed.
My eyes will flow unceasingly, without relief,
until the Lord looks down
from heaven and sees."

Lamentations 3:48-50

CONTENTS

ACKNOWLEDGMENTS

This book would not have been possible if it hadn't been for my very patient and gracious friend Bob Abbott. He was able to walk in my shoes and understand my feelings because of his love for Muslims that grew out of the war years he lived through in Beirut, Lebanon. Bob, I sincerely thank you.

A special word of thanks also to Juanita Abbott, who so generously gave of her husband's time and who also typed the first drafts of the manuscript.

I am very grateful to Sue Montgomery, who patiently edited the manuscript and faithfully coordinated this project to its completion.

My special thanks to Carol Johnson, editorial director at Bethany House Publishers, and her staff for the valuable insights they gave us in writing this book.

I am indebted to several Afghan friends, who encouraged me to write about Afghanistan. One such friend in particular always encouraged us and never doubted that this book would someday become a reality.

I sincerely appreciate the words of encouragement I received from my friends Jerry Parsley and J. Philip Hogan who, before a line was ever written, encouraged Julie and me to share our experiences for the benefit of others.

The title was suggested by my German friend Guido (Guy) Braun. Thank you, Guy.

I am thankful to Ken Horn, who guided us through the process of the publication of the second edition.

Most of all, I'm grateful to my Savior, who has given me the privilege of sharing with others my love for Afghanistan. This book has been written for the glory of God alone.

When David sent me his manuscript and asked me to read it and consider writing the foreword, three things went through my mind. First, that I was very busy and didn't have a lot of time to be reading manuscripts. Second, that I had so much respect for David Leatherberry, if he wanted me to read his manuscript the matter was settled—I would make time to read it. And finally, that I was deeply honored that he would ask me to write the foreword.

After settling my initial thoughts, I began reading the manuscript. By the second page, I was hooked and couldn't put it down.

David and Julie Leatherberry are unusual people. I remember a question he asked me several years ago: "Why are some people not flat out for God?" Indeed this was a very real question in his mind and he was genuinely perplexed. In southern lingo, "flat out" means giving it the best you've got ... holding nothing back. Knowing David, I understood why he would ask such a question. He has never been anything but "flat out for God." For David and Julie, it's a lifestyle. I'm sure it is a puzzle to them as to why every Christian doesn't live like that.

If you have a question about what "flat out for God" really means, read this book. It will clear it up for you. David and Julie follow God's call into the valley of the shadow of death, literally laying their lives on the line. In this case, the "valley" is Afghanistan during the Russian occupation. They are there because they love the people of Afghanistan and are willing to do whatever it takes to show forth the love of Christ. Like the apostle Paul,

David and Julie can say with deep conviction: "For me to live is Christ, and to die is gain."

Be prepared for one of the most exciting adventure stories you have ever read. Also be prepared to spend time in introspection when you finish reading it. *Afghanistan, My Tears* did two things for me. First, it caused me to ask myself how willing I am to lay it all on the line for God. Second, it gave me a fresh understanding of God's supernatural power to break down the walls of resistance I can't break down in pursuing His will for my life.

Having read this book, I am going to be a more effective follower of Christ. I would encourage every Christian and Muslim to read it. It will cause a fresh dedication in the lives of Christians. It will enable Muslim friends to understand what truly motivates people like David and Julie.

Among many there is a growing awareness today that a great spiritual awakening is on the way. It will happen where there are more David and Julie Leatherberrys who are willing to be "flat out for God."

—Jerry Rose
Former President
WCFC-TV 38 Chicago

Why This Book Was Written

On November 12, 1984, *CBS Evening News* Anchor Dan Rather gave the first of two up-to-date reports on the war in Afghanistan. Beginning with the communist coup in 1978, called the Saur Revolution, the war had become even more intense with the 1979 Russian invasion. Traveling alongside the Afghan Freedom Fighters, a CBS cameraman had taken intimate action footage of the conflict. Using a night vision camera, he was able to film what was claimed to be the largest sabotage operation of the war.

Blowing up high-voltage electrical lines, towers, and pylons that carried power to Kabul, the Fighters disrupted a basic service to the city—a common tactic in this kind of war.

Knowing at daybreak there would be retaliation from the air by the enemy, the guerrillas had helped people evacuate nearby villages before the power line attack. With bewilderment and anxiety etched on their faces, women, children, and old men had fled the homes where they had lived for generations. They left behind all but a few prized possessions, realizing the rest would be destroyed. Dan Rather stated the only time the cameraman saw the Fighters cry was that night.

As I watched those scenes flash across my television screen, I longed once again to be back in Afghanistan to see friends I hadn't seen for more than a year, to find out if they were even alive.

Near the end of the news report the following night, the camera zoomed in on a bearded, perspiring, 27-year-old Afghan Freedom Fighter who lay dying from a bullet wound to the back of the head. Within me, I sensed the frustration of his fellow Fighters. Though they dared to hope he would live, they knew it would soon be over. I watched as this brave young man clung to his last moments of life.

As the dying man moaned, I heard Dan Rather say, "This is the sound of victory."

His words unleashed within me the deepest sadness I had ever felt. It was as if a member of my own family had just died. For this lone Afghan symbolized a nation I knew and loved, a wounded and bloodied nation where noble people existed on raw courage.

Other images on my television screen replaced the report of the "forgotten war." Though the scenes from Afghanistan would quickly fade from the minds of most people, for my wife, Julie, and me the vivid pictures would not disappear.

Suddenly I knew I had to be alone. The scenes I had just witnessed would not go away. Even as I hurried from the room, I could still see the young man dying.

Alone in the next room, I fell to my knees to pray, but I could not speak. Tears from a well buried deep inside me could not wash the young Fighter's face from my mind. Hot tears of agony and the sweet hurt of memories mingled in my torn emotions. I felt unspeakable pain. Over and over the young man's face stabbed my consciousness and tore at me with the question: *Who cares? Who really cares for him, for Afghanistan?*

In my ears rang the cries of a thousand suffering people—cries unheard by the masses of the world. The weight of caring crushed me. Sobs and groans expressed my unutterable prayer for mercy. Never before did I realize that love could be so painful.

Then a new video began to play in my mind. I saw a Man being savagely beaten by the fists of others. The hatred of the men was obvious as they sneered and spat on the blindfolded Man. He twisted one way and then another as the blows smashed in from unseen sources. Part of the Man's beard was yanked out, leaving splotches of spittle and blood. Though the torture continued, He neither resisted nor tried to protect himself.

Through my mind's eye, I saw two men chain Him to a post. Then a third brawny man began lashing His back until blood ran.

Next I saw men driving nails into the beaten Man's hands and feet, securing Him to a cross. The cross was then raised and dropped into a hole in the ground with a gut-wrenching thud.

After some time, the Man on the cross pushed against His pinioned feet, filled His tortured lungs with air, and cried in a loud voice, "It is finished!" After those words, His entire body slumped.

A soldier who was walking by hesitated, then thrust a spear into the limp body hanging above him. Blood and water spilled to the ground.

Though the judge who had sentenced that Man to die could find no fault in Him, a hate-filled crowd demanded the Man be handed over to them. Now here He was, suspended by nails from a cross, His innocent blood staining the rough-hewn wood.

As I looked more closely, I saw that the bright afternoon sun had dried the blood and lighted a placard above the Man's head. The placard read: "Jesus of Nazareth."

As the scene ended and my mind returned to the present, I could feel the risen Christ's awesome, gentle presence. More than ever before I understood the depths of His great love. God had used the suffering of that Afghan to let me feel His suffering. He allowed me to see how very much He had given for the whole world, including that fallen warrior.

Everything I saw that day made me want to return to the Afghans once again, to give my life in service to them. I wanted to live with them and, if need be, to suffer with them.

As tears streamed down my face, I heard these words: *David, that's how I cry when I see people suffer like that.*

Those scenes and those words are what confirmed to me I should write this book. It is my sincere hope that through the words on these pages, others will see and come to love the hurting people of Afghanistan.

—David Leatherberry

A F G H A N I S T A N
A N D   I T S   N E I G H B O R S

1

EXPLODING AFGHANISTAN

In the pitch-black darkness, our lone jeep bounced along a blacktop Kabul street. Our taillights made strange, blood-red images in the trailing dust, and our headlights illuminated only a few yards of the deserted street. Without street lamps or even starlight, the dark buildings that lined each side of the street helped create a sense of fear. Our fear was not unwarranted. The strict curfew, invoked by the Afghan communist coup, had turned familiar streets into lonely gauntlets where death often struck with indiscriminate swiftness.

About us was nothing but extraordinary quietness. Standing in darkened shades of black and encompassed by a barbed wire fence, even the normally busy military installation was still. This too added to my foreboding. Only our noisy jeep broke the cold, nocturnal silence.

There were three of us in the jeep: My wife, Julie, Clifford Ronselle, and me. As a medical doctor, Clifford worked with a humanitarian project in Afghanistan. Julie and I helped with those efforts as well, dividing our time between that and an in-depth study of Pushtu, one of Afghanistan's two major languages.

There was just enough light in the dilapidated jeep for me to see my watch. As I glanced at it, I broke the thick silence and said, "Cliff, this is too close for comfort. It's 9:45 and they have permission to shoot on sight after 10 o'clock. Let's hope their watches are all correct. Can't you move this contraption a little faster?"

The young doctor looked down at the faintly glowing speedometer, then back to the road. "Better not," he replied, glancing quickly at me and giving me a reassuring smile. "It will make us look suspicious. We're the only ones on the street."

That I already knew, and I felt more than a little conspicuous!

Why didn't we leave sooner? I asked myself as I recalled the disconcerting rumors I'd heard earlier in the week about the guard who shot a driver because he didn't stop quickly enough, and about the young inexperienced soldier who "thought" he saw a weapon and fired.

Shaking my head to rid myself of these thoughts, I again broke the silence. "Cliff, we're crazy. It just occurred to me that we're riding in an old, gray, military-type jeep. Stop this thing," I said jokingly, "I want out." Turning toward Julie I asked, "How about you?"

"Good idea," she answered, not very convincingly. Apparently my joke was lost on her.

Cliff smiled again and said, "Hold on, Davey. We only have about five blocks to go and you'll be home safe and ...."

Before another syllable could be uttered, he slammed on the brakes with all his might. I pitched forward. The screeching tires almost instantly halted the sideways skid of the four-wheel-drive vehicle. In front of our jeep, less than seven feet from my face, was the muzzle of a rifle. I expected to see fire explode from the barrel before I could even exhale. The soldier stood alone in the middle of the road, aiming an AK-47 at us. I pushed my upraised hands hard against the rough, steel top of the jeep and dared not blink my watering eyes. I was afraid even the slightest movement would be perceived as aggression and provoke him to shoot us without hesitation. With our hands frozen in position and our hearts pounding, we waited while the young soldier studied us.

My thoughts raced: *What's the problem? It's not 10 o'clock yet. He looks like a nice boy a mother would be proud of. Please don't ...*

Suddenly he moved, tilting his head to peer into the backseat. When he ascertained we were foreigners, he eased his position ever so slowly and stepped to the side of the jeep. Then without a word, he waved us on with the muzzle of his weapon. In unison, we meekly nodded our heads.

Cliff put the jeep in gear and eased it down the road. He took a deep breath and exhaled forcefully. I slumped in my seat, and Julie closed her eyes.

"Are you okay?" I asked Julie.

"I'm fine, David," she answered.

"How about you, Cliff? Are you okay?" I asked.

He looked straight ahead and gripped the steering wheel for a moment. In a voice higher pitched than usual he said, "Yeah, I'm all right." Then clearing his throat he more firmly declared, "I'm fine." I wasn't sure if he was trying to convince me or himself.

No one spoke until we arrived in front of our house. "Cliff, come on in and stay with us," I said. "There's only eight minutes before the curfew begins."

"No thanks. I can make it home in five minutes or so."

"Are you sure?"

"Yeah, I'm sure. Besides, I think I want to go home and

start packing for Alabama. I'll call you later."

Cliff pulled the noisy vehicle away and accelerated quickly. I watched the taillights brighten as he braked and turned right. As he disappeared around the corner, I whispered, "Watch over him, Lord."

"Amen," Julie added.

Inside our house, Julie asked, "Do you think Cliff was joking about packing his bags for Alabama?"

"Well, after tonight, I'm sure he's seriously considering it," I replied. "Afghanistan has become a dangerous place. Who knows what will happen next?"

"I sure don't," she said. "Do you want me to fix a bite to eat? This excitement has made me hungry."

"Good idea," I answered.

Julie went into the kitchen and I rested my head against the back of my favorite chair, letting my mind wander over the events of the last two weeks.

On the night of April 17, 1978, Mir Akbar Khyber, a prominent communist leader, was gunned down by unknown assailants. On April 19, more than 10,000 communists and sympathizers went to Khyber's house in the Microyan section of Kabul to receive his body for a funeral procession that would proceed across part of the city.

After they made a relatively quiet march to the burial site, a fiery, anti-imperialist demonstration took place near the center of Kabul at Zarnagar Park. Marxist leaders shouted their enthusiastic speeches through harsh-sounding bullhorns and public address systems. The noisy gathering was punctuated with slogan shouting and upraised fists. For many people, it was chilling to see so many boisterous youth, some wearing red armbands, chanting Marxist slogans of atheistic materialism in Kabul, an

Islamic city diametrically opposed to such an ideology.

I had heard about the communists' activities at Kabul University and in some high schools, but I suspected they propagandized their strength. A number of military officers were Moscow-trained, but I could not picture communism dissuading Afghans from their firm belief in God. However, the Russians' interest in Afghanistan was obvious from the imposing, two-block-long embassy area, sitting fortress-like behind highly guarded and intimidating walls.

After the demonstration, the tension filling the air caused people to wonder what the Afghan government or the communists might do. Many were very surprised by the Marxists' strength.

In the very early morning hours of April 26, a government crackdown put some key communist leaders in jail. However, one of their main spokesmen, Hafizullah Amin, was only placed under house arrest. According to some reports, that proved to be a costly mistake for Afghanistan's President Daoud. It is believed that during the few hours that passed before Amin was finally taken to jail, he set in motion the coup that would begin on the 27th.

By midmorning on April 27, our neighborhood came alive with rumors about trouble downtown, but we saw and heard nothing. In the afternoon, however, Julie and I watched two jet fighters begin cutting crisp circles high above Kabul.

With great concern in her voice, Julie asked, "What are those planes for?"

Since there had been a great deal of talk about a student-led, antigovernment demonstration at the Presidential Palace, I suggested the planes were a show of strength by the government. However, my assumption soon proved to be wrong. With deadly swiftness, the jets suddenly dropped straight down, came in low over the edge of the city, and fired two rockets toward the military base outside Kabul near Kargha Lake.

I bounded up the stairs of our home and out onto the balcony. From there I could clearly see the two high-flying planes slicing the brilliant blue sky. In open-mouthed wonder, I focused first on the planes, then on the place where the rockets disappeared. Julie came to the balcony in time to see grayish smoke rising from the rocket strikes. A helpless, sinking feeling washed over me.

Later, other planes flew into our city from four directions. One after the other, they dove and fired on the Presidential Palace before knifing upward. As they circled directly overhead, I could plainly see the rockets still remaining on their wings. The thought of the resulting death from each pass made me feel ill. However, unable to conquer my fascination, I continued to watch the air strikes. Soon the peaceful blue sky became dirty and angry-looking from the rising black smoke and the gray vapor trails that crisscrossed it with every turn of the jets.

I later learned that the administrators at Malalai High School, a French-sponsored, all-girls school located a few blocks west of the Presidential Palace, decided to dismiss their students at about 11:30 that morning. They were greatly concerned by the tension in the area and wanted to send the girls home before anything happened. However, neither the early discharge nor the recent rumors and antigovernment demonstrations were of particular concern to two of the school's students as they left the building that day.

Spogmay, the 16-year-old daughter of Mr. Munsif, our language teacher, and her friend Gwooljan casually strolled east along the street toward the palace, happy to have been dismissed early. Spogmay's petite build, bouncy, shoulder-length hair, and soft, almost mysterious smile were a great contrast to her friend Gwooljan's tall stature, waist-length hair, and explosive giggle.

The girls, best friends, intended to catch a bus at the stop near Pushtunistan Square. As they passed Zarnagar Park, they could sense the excitement in the air as people crowded the streets—especially the streets close to the palace. The imposing residence of the president and the government headquarters buildings dominated the entire area. As usual, from the high square tower of the arched main gate the proud flag of the Republic of Afghanistan gently waved in the breeze.

"Why are there tanks? And why are the jeeps full of soldiers?" Spogmay asked as they neared the square.

"Maybe it's some military practice," Gwooljan replied. "Aren't the flowers in the barrels of the rifles cute?"

The girls threw back their heads and laughed. Their spirits seemed to match that bright, sunny April day.

Gwooljan suggested they watch for a while, so the girls walked in front of the Kabul Hotel and stood on the north side of the Telephone Exchange Building facing the street. Across the street, people were having lunch at the Khyber Restaurant.

Suddenly a blast erupted from a tank. Startled, the people looked up but no one moved. Then more tank shells exploded, firing on the palace. Restaurant patrons jumped up, overturning tables as they fled the building. Pedestrians started running, and cars raced to get away.

As jittery soldiers began shooting in all directions,

people began to fall on the street and the sidewalks. Some were killed instantly; others lay on the ground writhing in pain. Those who could, tried to get back on their feet and run.

Amid the panic, Spogmay also began to run. A boy about 12 years of age ran beside her until bullets cut him down. At a glance, Spogmay saw a beautiful yellow flower near the young boy's hand.

Terrified, Spogmay increased her speed, but stumbled slightly as one of her shoes went flying. *Where shall I go?* she thought.

Turning away from the tanks and soldiers, she began sprinting toward an open door screaming, "Gwooljan! Where are you?" Receiving no answer, she threw herself headlong through the door, rolled over the dirty floor, and came to rest on the far side of the room. As she turned back toward the door, she saw Gwooljan quickly duck inside to safety.

With tears streaming, the scraped and disheveled girls hugged one another.

"If we stay here we'll be trapped, Gwooljan!" Spogmay yelled. "We have to leave."

On bruised hands and knees, the girls crawled out the door and down the street to the next shop. From there they crouched and ran from store to store until they were finally far enough away from the smoke and confusion to stop and rest against a wall.

Between gasps for air Gwooljan sobbed, "What's going on? What's happening?"

Spogmay said, "I have no idea. I just want to go home."

Toward evening, the unmistakable sound of shots from rifles and machine guns sent Julie and me into the innermost room of our house for safety. After nightfall we hung blankets over our windows to prevent flying glass from hitting us.

Huddled in blackness near the radio, we listened as the station broadcast a lot of political rhetoric but precious little real information. Still, it provided us with a link to the fury outside.

From every direction we heard the sound of machine gun fire disrupting the quiet of the night. Around midnight, one of the decisive tank battles began four blocks from our home. Each loud blast of cannon fire shook the earth, causing our little house to tremble. We put our mattress on the floor and lay down. Too concerned to sleep, Julie and I spent the time talking and praying for our Afghan and international friends.

Who is fighting whom? Are our friends and colleagues caught in this firestorm? Will air strikes begin again at dawn? In my mind I asked these questions of the unanswering darkness.

Facedown on the floor with my head resting on my arm, I felt a deep, inner ache for the people nearby who were being wounded and killed.

Daylight broke to the whine of jets splitting the sky and the sound of exploding rockets rolling like thunder across Kabul. While still on the mattress in the middle of the floor, we suddenly heard a screaming jet plunge over our house.

Instinctively I jerked a sheet over Julie's head and yelled, "This is it, Baby!"

I just knew a wing missile was targeted for our home. But the jet roared past.

Grinning sheepishly, I uncovered Julie's head and said, "All clear."

With a twinkle in her eye she replied, "Thank you, Sir Galahad."

Several hundred, perhaps thousands of people died during those horrible 19 hours. Most were soldiers much too young to handle those large, automatic weapons of death they held. Many people perished because their curiosity had drawn them to the streets where they were caught in a nightmare of crossfire or shot accidentally by the nervous, inexperienced soldiers.

Afghanistan was exploding.

Shortly after the coup ended that day, we found our telephones still worked. Concerned deeply about our friends, I called across Kabul to the Munsif home. Mr. Munsif's son Amir answered.

"*Asalaam alekum* (Peace be upon you)," he said.

"*Wali kum salaam* (And peace be upon you also)," I responded.

Forcing my voice to sound calm, I asked, "Are you and your family okay?"

"We're okay," he replied. "Spogmay was downtown when the fighting broke out, but she got home safely. Thank God."

"Yes indeed, thank God. Please stay inside," I urged.

"We will," he said.

"Is your father still in Jalalabad?" I asked.

"Yes, he's there," Amir replied. "He'll be worried about us."

Understanding Amir's concern, I answered, "Yes, I know. Julie and I will be praying for your family and for him."

"Thanks," he replied.

Not knowing what else to say, I said, "Call if we can do

anything for you."

"Don't worry, Daoud," Amir said, using the Pushtu name for David. "We'll be okay. You and Julie be careful yourselves."

"We will," I assured him.

"Let's try to stay in touch," he said.

After I promised we would do so, Amir closed the conversation by saying, "May God keep you."

"And you too," I replied.

There was nothing else we could do, but we were comforted, knowing our prayers could make the difference for the Munsif family and for others in Afghanistan who had become such beloved friends.

Because they had no telephone, we could not contact our language helper, Ajmal Masoude and his family. Therefore, the day after the coup, although things were still very tense and uncertain, I risked a brief stop at the Masoude family's shop. I was relieved to see the heavily-whiskered, square face of Rahman. His thick mustache seemed to jump as he smiled broadly and firmly shook my hand.

"Good to see you, Daoud," he said.

"Same here, Rahman," I replied.

Calling to his younger brothers, Rahman said, "Come quickly; Daoud is here."

The first to appear was 17-year-old Ajmal, bright-eyed and alert as usual. The slender, smooth-faced youth had the look of a serious student, especially with his large, black-rimmed glasses and short clipped hair.

"I'm glad you're okay, Daoud," he said.

"And you too, my friend," I replied.

Before I finished speaking, Khadim came in. Quietly he said, "Hello, Daoud. How are you?" Tallest of the three, this gentle brother smiled, accenting the small mole just to the right of his thin, immature mustache.

"Julie and I are both fine and I'm happy to see you three. Is everyone in your family okay?" I asked. My heart stopped as I waited for his reply.

"Yes," he responded.

"Are you sure? How is your brother-in-law who is stationed near Kargha Lake?" I inquired.

"We don't know," Khadim replied. "We have had no word from him yet."

"Julie and I are praying much for him, that God will bring him safely to you," I said.

"Thank you. Thank you very much," the brothers said, almost in unison. Their faces were very solemn.

I tried to think of a better way to relieve their fears. The Masoudes had practically made Julie and me part of their family. "God has helped us in the past and He can do it again," I said. "I must be going now, but please be careful."

"You too, be careful," said Ajmal.

"May God keep you," I replied.

"May God be with you," answered the brothers.

These brief conversations seemed overshadowed with the uncertainty of the times, making them strained and at times halting. It was as though we wanted to say more, but what more could we say? Chitchat, levity, and even smiles seemed out of order. Yet this type of somberness was very unusual in our normal conversations.

Two days after the coup the telephones quit working, so I took a cab across town to check on the Munsif family once again. Afraid I would bring the Munsifs trouble because I was a foreigner, I did not go directly to their house. Instead I got out of the taxi a couple of streets away.

"Lord, make a way for me to find out if the Munsif family is okay," I prayed.

Almost instantly Amir appeared on his bike and pulled up alongside me. The tall, lanky teenager gave me a weak smile. Beads of perspiration had wet his wavy hair and come to rest atop his thick eyebrows.

Not waiting for him to catch his breath, I asked, "Is everyone okay?"

"We're all fine, David," he replied.

"Great!" I said, quickly glancing around. "Your father?"

"He made it home and is fine," Amir answered.

"We shouldn't talk longer," I said.

"Yeah, it's a bad situation right now," he agreed.

"I know. We are praying," I said. "Contact me when it's safe enough, okay?"

"We will," Amir responded as he shoved off.

His bike swayed from side to side with the forceful thrust of his legs. As I watched him disappear, I was flooded with thankfulness that my teacher and his family were safe.

As time wore on, the coup brought many visible changes to the city of Kabul but even more change to the spirits of its people. A deadly sense of peril took hold and fear permeated the streets, bringing distrust and suspicion, even in the daylight hours. No one dared entertain a foreigner, and friends were unable to freely greet each other publicly. Worst of all, people began disappearing, never to be seen or heard from again.

Suddenly the Afghans couldn't be Afghan. Centuries of hospitable traditions by a warm and friendly people were shut off by a terrible sense of fear. The present, fear-bound city stood in marked contrast to the Kabul we had moved to in 1976. It felt strange living amid suspicion and fear, to have to move about with such caution. But that was how it was. Traditional Afghan life and independence had exploded and disappeared on the day of the coup.

My reminiscing ended when Julie returned from the kitchen. The color that had left her face during the traumatic jeep ride had returned.

She carried tuna sandwiches, sliced tomatoes, and hot tea over to the coffee table and set them down. Turning to me she asked, "How long do you think they will allow us to stay here?"

For a moment I didn't answer. Finally I replied, "I don't know, but the government has certainly become anti-American."

"But we are followers of Christ and care about people," Julie said. "We are here to help, not hurt anybody."

"I know, but explain that to the communists," I responded.

"We are here because of God's love. In fact, showing His love is needed now more than ever. Didn't your heart go out to that scared young soldier tonight?"

"Yes, it did, once I found it again," I replied. "But I'm not certain what we should do. The situation has drastically changed. For our Afghan friends to associate with us now is to endanger their lives. Do we have the right to do that? Yet how can we abandon them when they are hurting the most?"

"What a dilemma," Julie said slowly.

I walked over and sat down on the couch by Julie. As I took her hand, we began to talk about the events that had brought us to Afghanistan.

"God has always given us guidance," I said. "Only He can make known to us what our response should be."

As Julie and I ate our snack, my thoughts turned to my first encounter with Him.

2

GET OUT OF MY LIFE

My hometown, Bristolville, Ohio, sits on the crossroads of State Highway 88 and U.S. 45—10 miles from the big auto and steel town of Warren. When I was growing up, Bristolville boasted a grocery store, a park, a hotel with a beer garden (which I was afraid to go near), a doctor's office, and my special place, Deemers—a forerunner of the modern convenience store. At Deemers men met to talk about how well the high school basketball team was doing, would do, or had done. And when Dad bought gas there I could get a good "ice cream comb" and the latest cowboy comic book.

My family lived on Route 45 about a mile north of the town square. Alongside the driveway near a group of trees, Dad made a sandbox. Each spring he filled the box with new white sand. We also had a long swing hung from a big oak tree near the house. Sometimes I would sit on the swing, look up the long ropes, and listen to them squeak as I pushed myself back and forth, scuffling my feet along the narrow bare spot in the green lawn. Other times I would just sit and let the breeze slowly push me. Often I would sit there and wait for my dad to come home from the steel mill, or for my sister Eloise to come from school on the big yellow bus.

One day, the summer before I started school, I was in the basement of our little bungalow riding my tricycle.

My "engine" roared as I pedaled my racer as fast as my legs could move. I went through one of the doorways and around the big ugly furnace. Getting faster and bolder with every turn, I tore past the coal bin and went flat out on the straightaway. My tires screeched as I made the turn by the bright sunbeam that slanted in through the small smudged window. Then I barreled triumphantly through the other doorway with the cheers of an imaginary crowd filling my ears.

I was having a great time, unhindered by the adult world upstairs, when unexpectedly I felt I should get quiet. I got off my tricycle and stood beside it, completely still.

It seemed as if my mom was praying, except she wasn't there. But I knew that the Lord Jesus was there and I dropped my head reverently.

At that moment I felt the guilt of my childish wrongs and knew I needed to ask Jesus to forgive me. I remained quiet for a few moments, and then said, "Dear Jesus, I'm sorry." The moment I spoke those words, warm joy spread over me and tears came to my eyes. "Thank You," I whispered.

The presence of Jesus was so real I didn't move for a long time. I was concerned I would bump into Him, yet my feelings of awe and wonder weren't fearful. I was totally at peace. After a few more minutes, I felt free to go upstairs.

"Mom," I called as I reached the top of the stairs.

"Yes, Davey," she said, turning from the sink and wiping her hands on a towel. She focused her soft blue eyes on me and smiled, waiting for me to speak.

I didn't know how to explain what I'd just experienced, but since Mom never laughed at anything I told her, I began.

"Jesus was here," I said.

"What do you mean?" she asked.

"Well, He just came," I answered.

"And," she continued, waiting for me to say more.

"I felt bad and I told Him I was sorry," I answered. "He came, Mom, and I said I was sorry. And He forgave me, Mom. Then I told Him, 'Thanks.'"

Acting as if what I told her was the most natural thing in the world, she hugged me and planted a kiss on my forehead. "I'm glad, Davey," she said.

Autumn brought great excitement as I entered the first grade. When the big yellow bus stopped at our house that first day, its flashing lights seemed to blink, *Hurry ... hurry.* After I said good-bye to my 2-year-old sister, Violette, Eloise took my hand and helped me cross the road. We made our way around the bus's shiny front bumper and up the big stairs. Walking down the black rubber aisle, we sat down on one of the smooth seats. I tightly held the new treasures I had brought with me for my first day of school. I was proud of my new lunch box. It was decorated with a cowboy picture. I also had a brand-new pencil and an orange box of crayons.

I wiggled to sit up as tall as possible so I could see out the window. After the bus driver closed the doors, the bus began to move. *At last,* I thought, *I'm going to school.*

Soon the falling snow of winter replaced the beautiful falling leaves of autumn. Coloring pictures for my mom and learning the ABC's competed with snowball fights for excitement that year.

Almost before I knew what was happening, the aroma of fresh-baked cookies and the sound of carols filled our home, announcing Christmas was fast approaching. Childish anticipation over the soon-to-be received presents mounted with each passing day.

What will I get this year? I wondered as I looked at the growing mound of brightly wrapped gifts under the tall, beautifully decorated tree.

Though it seemed as if Christmas morning would never arrive, it finally did. Eloise, Violette, and I jumped out of bed and raced for the gifts. I soon had each one that was marked "Davey" in front of me. Pushing aside the smaller packages, I unwrapped the biggest one first. It was the most beautiful toy car I had ever seen—a shiny white convertible with real mirrors, white sidewall tires, and a red interior. When I'd spin the wheels and let it go, it would race across the floor with the sound of a smooth whir. Though I liked my other gifts, none compared with my new car.

On the first day back in school following our Christmas vacation, my teacher, Mrs. Brown, asked us to tell what we had received for Christmas. Immediately I raised my hand as high as I could. I wanted to tell about all the wonderful gifts I had received, but I especially wanted to talk about my car. However, Mrs. Brown decided to go around the room row by row so I had to wait my turn.

In the first row next to the window, about the fourth seat back, sat a boy named Albert. When it was his turn, Mrs. Brown said, "Albert, what did you receive for Christmas?" When Albert didn't say anything, Mrs. Brown asked him again.

Finally, holding up a single row, 10-cent box of crayons, he haltingly answered, "This box of crayons."

"And what else did you get for Christmas?" Mrs. Brown asked.

"That's all," Albert said. His face turned red.

I thought about the many toys I had received and the great times I had had playing with them. Thinking about Albert's single gift, I lost my enthusiasm to talk about all the things I had received. In fact, I was relieved when my turn was over.

Throughout the day all I could think about was Albert. He usually came to school in the same shabby clothes that always needed to be washed and pressed. He had one droopy eyelid, and often his face needed washing. I particularly noticed his dirty ears because my mother always checked mine to be sure they were clean. *His mother must not check his,* I often thought. Albert wasn't as smart as most of the kids in our class, so the other children would play tricks on him and make fun of him.

That night, after kneeling by my bed and saying my prayers with my mom, I snuggled down in the warm covers but I couldn't sleep. Once again I recalled Albert's unsmiling face and the box of crayons. Since that day in the basement, I would often talk to Jesus when I was alone. That night I began talking to Him about Albert: "Jesus, what about Albert? He doesn't have much. Jesus, what are You going to do about Albert?"

A reply quickly came to my mind: *David, what are you going to do about Albert?*

Me? What can I do? I thought. Then an idea suddenly sprang into my mind. I knew what I could do; I could give Albert one of my toys. That would make Jesus and Albert both happy.

I reviewed my new toys one by one, finally selecting a small plastic cowboy mounted on a horse. "Jesus," I said, "I'm going to give Albert one of my cowboy toys."

As I waited under the covers for a commendation, there

was nothing but silence. Finally a question came.

Why not give your best toy?

My very best? I knew exactly which one He was referring to—my super-duper, white convertible.

How can I part with that? I thought. I loved playing with that car. It was my dream car and I handled it with special care.

Then I considered all I had and all Albert did not have. I could imagine how excited he would be to have such a car.

Finally I said, "Okay, Jesus, I'll give my best toy to Albert."

I knew I'd better talk with my mother about my decision since I would need her permission to give it away, so I slipped out of bed and quietly walked into the living room. My mother was sitting in a big stuffed chair. As I entered the room, she looked up, surprised to see me.

"Mommy," I said, "I have been talking with Jesus and He wants me to give my best toy to Albert."

Then I told my mother about Albert and what had happened that day at school.

When I finished, Mother said, "You know, Davey, if you give your best toy to Albert, a week or two from now you cannot ask for it back and we can't replace it. So, Davey, go back and talk with Jesus again and make sure this is what He is saying to you."

"Okay, Mom," I said. I went back into my room, pulled the covers up over me, kept my eyes wide open, and said, "Jesus, Mom said I should talk with You again about Albert and make sure You said I should give my best toy to him."

You should, came the answer.

"Thanks!" I told Him, and I jumped out of bed and ran

out to the living room.

"Mom," I said, "I'm sure Jesus wants me to give it. Please can I give my car to Albert?"

Mom replied, "Sure, Son, you can. I'll help you get it ready in the morning."

My mother had dedicated me to God even before I was born, and she prayed for me continually. If she was ever surprised by what I said about my conversations with God, she wisely kept her thoughts to herself. This allowed me to develop a natural and close relationship with God.

The next morning I awoke full of anticipation. Though giving away my car pained me somewhat, thinking about how I would surprise Albert brought excitement to my heart. Mom found a green cardboard tomato box with a handle in the middle, and my car fit into it perfectly.

On the way to school I thought about how and when I would give the car to Albert. I decided it would be best to wait until right before school was out that day. I knew Albert could easily be tricked, and I was concerned that someone would cheat him out of the car if I gave it to him any earlier. It would be hard to wait all day, but on the other hand I could still look at it and play with it at recess times. Throughout the day, everyone admired my shiny car.

The bell that rang five minutes before the dismissal bell warned us it was time to get our coats and line up. I picked up my box and took one long, last look at my beautiful car. Then I walked over to Albert.

"Albert," I said, "I have a gift for you. I want you to have my car."

Albert looked at me in disbelief.

"Here, please take it. It's yours," I said, trying to hand it to him. Still he would not reach out his hand to take it.

Instead he backed away and turned sideways, eyeing the car.

"It's really yours, Albert," I said again. I wanted him to know I wasn't pulling a mean trick on him. Carefully he reached for the handle, half expecting me to jerk it back. When he had it in both hands, he didn't know what to say, but a beautiful grin broke across his face.

The children who were nearby heard me and began talking with each other.

"David's giving his car to Albert," one said. They gathered around, looking at the shiny car in Albert's hands.

Pretty, well-dressed Karen said, "David, why didn't you give me your car?"

Why does she, who has so much, want Albert's gift? I thought. Her attitude upset me.

Frightened that someone might try to take the car from him, I stood close to Albert.

When the teacher appeared and asked why we hadn't lined up, someone said to her, "David gave his fancy car to Albert."

She looked at the box Albert was holding. After pausing for a moment, she then looked at me and asked, "David, did you give your car to Albert?"

"Yes, Mrs. Brown," I replied.

"Did your mother give you permission to give your car away?"

"Yes, Mrs. Brown."

"Are you sure?" she persisted.

I felt desperate. I knew she suspected I was not telling the truth, so with all the sincerity I could muster I said, "Yes, Mrs. Brown. I asked my mother and she said I could give it to Albert."

"Okay," she said slowly. I knew she still had her doubts,

and I was relieved that she let Albert keep the car.

We put on our coats and stood in line, waiting for our bus numbers to be called. When I heard "Number One," I bolted out the door. Then I stopped and looked back. Albert was standing there clutching his new treasure with bright eyes and a wide smile.

Suddenly I felt a deep happiness welling up inside of me and I began to choke up. I pressed my lips hard together and blinked. I hadn't known that giving could make you so happy. I thanked Jesus and whispered, "Albert is happy, Jesus. I'm glad I gave him my car." Going down the concrete steps of the school, I prayed, "Jesus, please don't let anyone take that car away from Albert."

Our family faithfully attended church in Warren, Ohio, where Reverend Caldwell was pastor. His only son, Noel, became my best friend and ideal. Since I was a mere 9-year-old and he was an obviously cool 12-year-old, I looked up to him with great admiration. In another setting, the difference in our ages might have separated us, but here it did not.

Noel was a stable believer who followed Christ faithfully. He taught me to dream big. We spent hours creating dreams and making promises to each other—not little promises either. The promises we made were forged by time and honor. We vowed we would always be at each other's important life events. Even after the Caldwells moved away, Noel and I remained best friends.

When I was 14, my Christmas present was a round-trip bus ticket from Warren, Ohio, to Columbia, South Carolina, where Reverend Caldwell was pastoring at that time. Wanting very much to visit Noel, I had asked my parents several weeks earlier if I could have the ticket instead of any other gifts. Though it was a bit of a sacrifice, they agreed. Tingling with anticipation, I looked forward to Christmas vacation and my big solo adventure.

Finally the day arrived when I was to leave. Dad drove me to the bus station and helped me get my ticket.

As I climbed the steps of the bus, I turned and said, "Thanks a lot, Dad." He nodded as the door closed.

I settled into the soft seat of the bus and listened to the steady rhythm of the highway as we sped along. When the excitement that initiated the 700-mile journey finally subsided, my mind began to wander.

I watched the farms and small-town scenery roll by and thought: *Will I be a businessman some day?* When a patrol car passed the bus with its red lights flashing, I wondered: *How about a state trooper? Or maybe I'll be a sailor like the young man three rows up; he looks pretty sharp.*

I shifted in my seat, looked at a picturesque, white-steepled church we were passing, and thought of Noel's dad. *No, I couldn't be a preacher,* I thought. *God has to specifically call you to be that. Besides, anything that takes college is out.*

Having arrived at that conclusion, I leaned back and closed my eyes for a nap.

When I awoke, I munched on sandwiches and celery Mom had sent and watched the people around me. The miles continued to roll by between our intermittent stops at filling stations and country stores. It was nightfall when I finished my last cookie and fell asleep.

The next morning I arrived at my stop and got off the bus. After collecting my suitcase, I walked the four blocks to Reverend Caldwell's church. I opened the door, and went in.

"Well, David!" Reverend Caldwell boomed in his big, exciting voice. "How nice to see you." He gave me a bear hug and said, "Let me call Noel. He'll be happy to see you."

Soon Noel was standing in front of me.

"Leatherbritches!" he exclaimed. "Great to see you!"

"You don't know how great it is to be here!" I replied.

He grabbed my big suitcase and we walked the short distance to his house. We spent hours catching up on things and recalling the old days. Later he introduced me to a cute girl, but I was too shy to talk to her. Anyway, South Carolina is too far away, I reasoned.

Sunday we went to church, but Reverend Caldwell wasn't preaching that day. The speaker was a young graduate student from Columbia Bible College. As I listened, I thought he spoke quite powerfully for his age. *He seems earnest and sincere in his desire to serve God,* I thought.

Noel and I sat near the back on the left, and my thoughts began to wander. I recalled times in Ohio when Noel and I would sit together in church, looking ever so pious, while secretly grasping hands as hard as we could to see who had the strongest grip. We would sit unflinching as our knuckles turned white. Finally, one of us would yield to the pain. I also thought about the endless hours of talk and laughter we had so enjoyed, and about the many times we had gone fishing but had never caught anything.

I finally brought my wandering thoughts back to the present and listened as the young student made his final point. It was then something powerful began to happen. I strongly sensed God's presence. In those last brief moments of the sermon and benediction, a deep, firm awareness took hold of me: I, David Leatherberry, was to enter the ministry.

Because those moments were too sacred for words, I
didn't say anything to anyone. What exactly my calling
meant or where I'd go, I didn't know; but that I had been
called into the ministry was crystal clear.

My stay in South Carolina ended all too quickly.
Though I was sad to leave my friend, my thoughts returned to my experience in Reverend Caldwell's church
almost as soon as I was seated on the bus. During the
long ride home I thought about my call from God. *How
swiftly that call came to me*, I thought. But I was confident and sure about His calling, and the assurance God
gave me felt like a warm coat in a winter storm.

The following summer Noel graduated from high
school. Not long after his graduation, I learned about
his plans to get married the next February. I was excited
about his upcoming wedding because it meant I would see
Noel once again. After all, as youngsters we had promised
to be at each other's important events, so I knew I would
be asked to take part in his wedding.

During the time between my visit with Noel at Christmas and the announcement of his upcoming wedding,
I suffered some real disappointments in adult believers.
Those discouragements made the wedding invitation
from my trusted friend all the more important. I knew he
would not let me down.

I checked the mail each day for the invitation I was su-
premely confident would appear. Yet day after day, it did
not come. The day before Noel's wedding rehearsal I once
again walked out to the mailbox and took out the handful
of letters. As I leafed through the letters, bills, and adver-
tisements, my heart sank. No invitation. Thinking I had

perhaps overlooked it, I carefully went through each piece again. There had been no oversight. The invitation was not there.

Devastated and very angry, I stomped back into the house, flung the mail on the table, marched upstairs to my bedroom, and slammed the door.

"That's it, I'm finished," I said aloud. "My most trusted friend has let me down."

Then I addressed God. "God, if that's the way it is with Christians," I shouted, "I don't want any part of them, or You either. Just get out of my life. I don't need You. Leave me alone and get out of my life."

After making that speech to God, I took my hurt and anger and crawled into bed. Surprisingly I went right to sleep.

That night, I dreamed I could see Noel's room. The sunlight was streaming in through the window and I saw Noel on his knees by his bed. He was quietly praying. He appeared just as he had when I had visited him: tall and freckled-faced, with a shock of dark hair falling into his eyes. Yet as I looked closer, he seemed more mature. Somehow he also seemed stronger. I could see that his face was lined with concern as he knelt beside his bed.

I listened carefully to his words and soon realized he was praying for me.

When I awoke, I could sense the awesome, sweet presence of the Lord Jesus Christ.

I wanted to hide when I thought about the terrible audacity I had displayed in my earlier address to God. Quietly I said aloud, "Oh, Jesus, please forgive me for being so foolish. Please forgive me for my shameful behavior."

I waited before Him a long time, absorbing His strength and forgiveness. I had made a terrible mistake by allowing myself to focus on Christ's followers rather than on Him. I had blamed God for the actions of people. When people had failed me, I thought God had somehow failed me as well. Through this situation I came to realize I was always to keep my eyes first upon Christ, and not His followers. This simple realization brought consistency to my life, allowing me to love and trust people even though they may fail.

On the day of Noel's wedding, I asked my parents if I could make the nearly forbidden, expensive, long-distance call to South Carolina to congratulate him. Knowing how important this was to me, they said that I could.

The operator rang the Caldwell number and Noel answered.

"Hi, Noel. This is David," I stammered. I didn't really know what to say. I just wanted him to understand that I loved him and trusted him. But in my heart I still could not comprehend why he left me out of this important time in his life.

Before I could say anything else, Noel said, "David, why didn't you answer my letter? I've been waiting to see if you could be in my wedding. I've been expecting to hear from you. Just last night I had to get someone else to take your place."

Then he continued, "You know we always planned to be in each other's big events. I wrote you back in December."

Flushed with embarrassment, I mumbled my apologies. Then I congratulated him and his bride-to-be and hung up.

As I looked back through a bundle of seven-week-old Christmas mail, I found Noel's letter. *How could I have been so dumb?* I asked myself. *Why didn't I just check the mail more closely or call him earlier?*

That event was a turning point in my life. I could love and trust again. God had not failed me. I had failed God. When He forgave me, His love overwhelmed me. I wanted to share His love with other teenagers, yet a large question remained unanswered in my mind: *Can God really use an ordinary guy like me to make a difference in the lives of others?*

3

ONE STEP SHORT

It was 1959, my senior year at Howland High. With great anticipation I had waited for this school year to begin. This year would be different from all the others, I reminded myself continually. I could just feel it in my bones.

I had attended the Youth for Christ conference in Winona Lake, Indiana, the summer before. I became excited as I listened intently to other high school kids telling about how Christ had helped them to make positive contributions to their school life. Their testimonies allowed me to believe that I, David Leatherberry, could somehow serve Christ in my school as well. Though my other school years had been mediocre, God had given me a sense of expectancy about this one.

Maybe if I did something well, people would listen to me, I reasoned. Then my testimony for Christ would have punch.

In all my school years, I had never been outstanding in anything. My grades were not above average no matter how hard I tried. I was never in band, and I often wondered why I was in choir; I could hardly carry a tune. Athletic teams usually cut me during tryouts because I was not physically gifted either.

Every child strives to be important in his parents' eyes, and I was no different. My dad believed the way to make a child good was by continual correction. After all, a compliment might spoil a youngster. He had grown up under this type of treatment, so that was the treatment I received. All through grade school and beyond I desperately tried to do something—anything—well, just so I could please my father.

How excited I was when I tried out and made the seventh-grade basketball team. Though I was only on the third string, I was on the team! Finally, I thought, I would have a chance to make my dad proud.

Knowing I would play little or not at all in a real game, I started trying to talk Dad into coming to a practice. After much coaxing, he finally agreed.

On the appointed Saturday morning, we drove to the gym in silence. I could hardly contain my excitement. *Dad is going to see me play,* I thought happily.

During the practice I raced up and down the court as though it were the most important game of the season. I worked harder than I'd ever worked before. I didn't care if it was just practice; my dad and a few other parents were in the bleachers. I had an audience to play for and I was going to make the most of this opportunity. I leaped for every loose ball and rebound. Though I didn't score much, I hustled and did my part.

After practice I couldn't wait to see Dad. I showered quickly and ran out to our car. I was a skinny seventh-grader with wet hair and a happy heart, waiting for a word—any word—of commendation. Even a little show of pride or satisfaction for hard effort would suffice ... but none came.

The silence grew deafening. When I could stand it no longer, I looked over at Dad with a tentative smile on my face and asked, "What did you think?"

As I waited for an answer, my heartbeats measured the long seconds of silence that followed my outburst. But Dad just kept looking straight ahead.

After what seemed to be an eternity, he finally cleared his throat and said, "Well, those other guys were really good. What was your problem?"

Crushed, I hung my head. I could feel tears forming. Turning toward the window, I quickly flipped them away. As I bit my trembling lip, I decided I would never ask my dad such a question again. Yet I never stopped trying to live up to what I imagined he wanted me to be.

Those feelings followed me into my last year of high school. Somehow, though, I knew that final year was one of great promise. I believed strongly something good was going to take place.

The big news at the beginning of my senior year was that a student teacher from the former year, George Landis, had been hired to teach English and to be the new track coach. Howland hadn't had a track team for several years.

When I first saw Coach Landis, I was encouraged. He wasn't big, probably only 5'9" or 5'10", but he had a sinewy, athletic build. He had been a high school football and track star.

It wasn't long before everyone at school liked Coach. The girls at Howland swooned over his handsome olive skin and curly black hair, and the guys were impressed by how well he could run hurdles and dashes.

Long before the track season began, word was out among the students that anybody who tried out would make the team. There would be no cuts. To lose your sweat suit, the symbol of being on the team, you would have to quit. With a heart full of excitement and great anticipation, I signed up for the team. Maybe, I reasoned, I could somehow be a testimony for the Lord.

The team was made up of many upperclassmen like my-self—those with little or no previous experience in track or any other organized sport. Though the other coaches laughed at the looks of the team, Coach Landis stuck to his promise and no one was cut.

After our first meeting, I stopped Coach and asked to be excused from Thursday practice.

"The Youth for Christ Club meets Thursday after school," I said. "But I will do the workout routine after-ward by myself if it's okay."

"Fine," he said, without hesitation.

Just like that? Maybe it doesn't matter because he doesn't expect much from me anyway, I thought.

That first week of track, I walked quickly from my Thursday afternoon Youth for Christ meeting toward the locker room to change clothes. The other team members had finished their workouts and were getting ready to leave. As I approached the gym, Coach was standing by the open door of his car. He looked over the top of the car and studied me intently.

I felt awkward under his gaze. I wondered how he really felt about my doing Thursday workouts alone. Perhaps he would think I wasn't as committed to the team as I should be, that I'd take it easy. Or maybe he really didn't notice me that much. Perhaps it didn't make any difference what third-stringers did.

After a long pause, Coach smiled and said, "Hi, David. How are you?"

Nervously I answered, "Oh, I'm fine, Coach. Just on my

way to do my workouts. I had a Youth for Christ meeting this afternoon. I'll be sure to do all my workouts."

"Oh, I know you will," Coach said. "No problem."

Then he paused again, giving me his full attention. It was as if I was the only person in the world—me, of all people.

Finally he said, "David, you're doing just fine, you know, just fine. You're going to make a good 880 man. Don't worry, okay?"

"Okay," I answered casually, trying not to show how thrilling the impact of his words was.

He believes in me, I thought as I watched him slip into the seat of his car and drive away.

The chilly March air and a cold light rain hit my face as I worked out that afternoon. But with each lap I felt uplifted. As I ran around the track, my thoughts also raced: *Coach Landis actually remembers my name. He's not upset with me. He understands about YFC. He actually thinks I can be a good 880 man.*

As the steady thump of my track shoes rang in my ears, I prayed, "Lord, help me to be a winner for You, Coach, and the team."

Somehow, I just knew I would make the 15 points I needed to letter. I had no doubts whatsoever. I would be a winner.

As I continued running that day, I realized I'd forgotten to thank Coach Landis for his encouraging words. But somehow I had the feeling it wasn't necessary.

It didn't take too many practices before I felt comfortable as part of the team. The coach's smile always put me at ease, yet his soft brown eyes, which seemed to light up when he grinned, could be penetrating as well. Coach Landis was a Catholic with a strong belief in God. He had our respect, for he never used foul language or anger to either intimidate or motivate us.

Because two other 880 men were more talented, I ran third string. For me, it was always a minor miracle to cross the finish line. Years later I learned why running was so difficult. I had bronchiectasis in my left lung, a weakness I had apparently been born with.

It was always the wind sprints that got to me. That's when you run hard for 220 yards, jog briefly, then sprint another 220 yards. Long-distance runners, those who ran the 880 and up, were expected to complete this routine six times. I'd run hard until I was in pain, gasping for air. After a brief time to recover, I'd do it again. One of my worst problems was I ran like a duck—my feet turned out instead of in or straight. Though Coach and other team members tried to teach me to redirect my feet, I couldn't.

Every time I ran, I prayed for Coach and for every member of the team. Sometimes I jogged with Big Jim Nycum, our shot-putter. We called him Big Jim because he was 225 pounds of solid muscle. Jim was also a basketball star. He was quite a contrast to my 6-foot, 132-pound frame.

"Jim," I'd say, "if you died today, would you be ready to go to heaven?"

I knew I had better be ready to go if Jim was in a bad mood, because he could have put me out of this world in one fell swoop. Usually, though, he would just laugh and say, "Preach it to me, Davey. Preach it to me."

The track season progressed reasonably well. Participating on the team was a great effort for me, and I didn't make much progress. Yet, I enjoyed every minute of it. I was part of the team.

One afternoon in April Coach Landis reminded us Ursuline, a constant powerhouse school in our area, would be our next opponent. We also knew Ursuline was the school where Coach Landis had set a record in low hurdles as a student. We wanted to do especially well.

On the day of the meet, our enthusiastic, patched-up team met the veterans head-on. Throughout the meet, the score was close.

Coach Landis drew us into a huddle. "We're dead even with them," he said. "Our last two events, the pole vault and the 880, will make the difference. Do your best!"

The vaulters started their last pole-bending thrusts into the air about the same time we were getting ready for the 880. To relieve my tension I walked past the empty stands and glanced at the vaulters.

"Come on, man!" I shouted to Jim Frazier who stood facing the bar with his pole in his hand. He gave me a thumbs-up sign.

I liked to run the 880. It was my race. I just knew I could place and help our team win. Although I had never placed higher than fifth in any race, my goal was to place fourth in this one because that was the last spot that was awarded a point.

Dave Wise, who would later do great things at Kent State University in track, had just finished first in the mile. He came over to encourage me. Our team enjoyed special unity—a spirit inspired by the attitude of our coach, who treated everybody equally.

This race was important for the team, the coach, me, and, I felt, for Christ too. I desperately wanted to contribute. I walked around shaking my hands and then, one at a time, my legs. I bent over, stretched, stood up, and paced some more.

When a voice called, "880, line up," I walked to the line, suddenly conscious of my spindly legs and shortness of breath. The starter snapped shut his pistol. I took three breaths, breathing as deeply as I could, and bent over once more to stretch.

"On your mark." I stepped to the line on the inside lane.

"Get set." Coach's words were in my mind: *We're even. Do your best.*

Crack! The shot was fired; the race began.

Three runners had sprinted to the front by the end of the first turn. The rest of us were running together in a pack. Everyone's position was maintained for the first lap. Shortly into the second lap, my lungs began to burn, but I was feeling pretty good and had a nice rhythm going. Two runners in our group started to fade slightly on the back-stretch and continued to do so throughout the race.

As the last turn came into view, I was breathing heavily and a weakness began to creep down my legs. When we started the kick, there were three runners ahead of me I would never catch, one close behind me, and two others who trailed far back. It didn't take much calculating to know I only needed to stay in front of that one runner for less than 10 yards to make fourth place. Just one man for 10 yards. I could do it.

Landis' voice was in my ears. "Run hard! When your legs are screaming stop, that's when you turn it on!"

I strained with all my might, ignoring the sweat that stung my eyes and the fire that burned my lungs. Fourth place was within my grasp. I could feel it in the rhythm of my steps and the smooth pump of my arms.

This is it! This is it! I am flying, I thought.

Just then the runner behind me was suddenly shoulder-to-shoulder with me. We had about seven paces to go.

No! He won't do it! I determined in my mind. But even as I increased my effort, so did he. Step for step he matched me in perfect rhythm. *I can do it!* I kept telling myself. *Just a little more.* I gasped for air, clenched my teeth, and tightened my fists for one final assault on the finish line. I strained my whole body and stretched every muscle to the limit as I forced my toe to the line and flung my exhausted body across it.

Yet all of my last-second efforts were to no avail. I failed. I lost by one step and my team lost the meet by one point. I was one step short.

Dejection, like the black of midnight, blanketed me.

Though Coach Landis should have been disappointed, he didn't seem to be. He wasn't even upset by my inadequacy and failure, for he knew I had given all I had.

As he laid his hand on my shoulder, I exclaimed, "Oh, Coach, I wanted this for the team!"

"It's all right, David," he said.

Though I knew in my heart he meant it, I could not be consoled. *Oh God, I prayed about this race and did it for You. Why couldn't I make at least fourth place?*

My dreams vanished. I wasn't a winner. I was a fifth-place finisher.

In May, a few weeks before graduation, I was struggling as usual during a Saturday workout. I ran as hard as possible until I got so physically sick I left the field to vomit. Afterward I walked away from the track about 30 yards and sat on a hay bale. I wanted to be alone, but Coach Landis came over and sat down beside me.

Looking directly at me, he said, "David, I want you to know that some guys don't have the physical bodies for this, even though they give it all they've got. I know you try your best. In fact, I wish everyone I coach had the same kind of spirit you have. I want you to be aware that I know you are giving it everything and that's all a man can do."

Though his comments made me feel better, each time I lost an event the 15 points it took to letter got more and more improbable, and the big letter H for Howland slipped further and further away from my grasp. It wasn't long before I knew it was impossible for me to letter. I didn't have one single point, and the way things were going I probably wouldn't earn any during the remainder of the season. Yet Coach continued to encourage me.

Finally, the day arrived for the county championship meet. We blew out every team. Our score reached 78 points; our nearest competitor had less than half that number. What a proud day for our school. Coach Landis's no-cut team became county champions. In fact, we were the only sports team in our school to have a winning season that year.

How happy and proud I was to be part of the team. Though I hadn't contributed points, I had added spirit, encouragement, and an example of hard work.

The year-end awards assembly was always a highlight at school, but I looked forward to this year's event more than usual. Finally I was a team member—a member of a championship team no less. More than 700 students filled the bleachers and gym floor that morning. How excited I was as Coach Landis summoned our entire track team to the front. The principal presented Coach Landis with the big, gold championship trophy amid thunderous applause, whistles, and shouts. Cheerleaders waving orange

and black pom-poms yelled, "That's our team!" The deafening roar in the gym sounded beautiful to me.

With a hearty handshake and his familiar smile, Coach
Landis walked down the line and presented a small
trophy to each team member. Receiving my own trophy
that day was one of the brightest spots of my high school
experience.

The coveted H letters were then presented to Dave
Wise, Big Jim Nycum, Jim Frazier, and several others.
Though disappointed I had not lettered, I was thankful
just to stand up there with those guys.

It was quiet for a few seconds, then Coach Landis said,
"Now, will David Leatherberry ..."

The sound reverberated from the cement block walls
and stunned me. Shock would not allow my ears to receive this.

A mistake, a cruel mistake! I thought.

Speechless and unsure, I didn't move until the guy next
to me slapped me on the back and insisted I walk over to
Coach Landis. Since I was on the end, I had to walk by
every team member. They all knew I had not earned one
single point, let alone the 15 required to letter.

What will they think? I thought.

But as I walked past them, my embarrassment gave way
to joy. The team members were smiling and they all shook
my hand or patted me on the back, saying things like:
"Hey, man, that's terrific." "Great!" "Congratulations!"

Coach, in the manner I had come to expect, talked
directly to me as he shook my hand. Offering me the big
orange H, he said, "I want you to know, David, I'm not
just giving this to you. You earned it. Congratulations,
you lettered!"

I learned later Coach Landis had a great deal of

difficulty getting the necessary approval from the athletic department for my special letter. Somehow in the end he convinced them a third-stringer had given as much as he possibly could, and even though he hadn't earned a single point he had given enough to earn a letter.

How deeply I treasured that letter and trophy. Every time I looked at them they reminded me of the lessons I learned from Coach and from running on the team.

I'll always be thankful for Coach George Landis. He knew I was not track material but he gave me an opportunity to be part of a team when anyone else would have cut me. In his eyes my efforts were superior even when my performance was not. From a coach who was more interested in molding a young man's character than in winning a meet, I learned not to quit—even when it was painful to keep going.

After being on the Howland High track team, I thought about God's no-cut team. My Life Coach never takes anyone's sweat suit either. To get off His team, you have to quit. I purposed in my heart never to quit, but to letter for God with my life. It used to bother me I wasn't a gifted individual, but I decided God had made me the way I am for a purpose. Since He accepts me as I am, so do I. When I stopped comparing myself to others, I found a new freedom.

4

A SUMMONS SOUNDS

From the time I was 14 years old, I knew the Lord had called me into the ministry. Because I was concerned I might short-circuit God's plan by becoming romantically involved at 18, at the conclusion of my senior year I stopped dating the girl I could have easily fallen in love with.

Julie Parry, a senior classmate of mine, was a cheerful, perky, 5'1" brunette who had an unwavering commitment to Christ. In fact, this quiet but determined young lady was responsible for getting our Youth for Christ Club started at Howland High. Her delightful personality was stealing my heart.

It was tough to tell her that the YFC graduation banquet would be our last date, but I knew I must. After the banquet and a quiet ride to her home, we lingered on her front porch swing. Just before I left, we had a quiet prayer, asking that God's will would be done in both our lives.

That summer I found it difficult not to drive the mile and a half down the road to her house, but I stuck to my commitment and only went to say good-bye to Julie in September. She went east to Nyack College in New York and I left for Evangel College in Springfield, Missouri. While at college I dated other girls. However, even though I enjoyed their company, I could not forget the brunette at Nyack.

At the end of the summer of my sophomore year, Julie came home for two weeks. The day after she arrived, I drove down the hill to see her. As I walked to the door of her home, I wondered how it would be to see her again. *Will I still feel the same about her?* I wondered.

"Hi," she said, as she opened the door.

Very quickly my question was answered. My feelings about her hadn't changed at all. In fact, she was more attractive than ever.

I asked her how she was doing. I knew she had gone to college with only a hundred dollars, and I had often wondered how she had made it with so little to begin with.

She said God had provided, and I understood what she meant. I had started Evangel College with very little money as well, and for the first time in his life my dad was unemployed that year.

From the familiar porch swing we talked about college life.

"Do any dating at school?" I inquired. *Why does that question make me nervous?* I thought, even as I voiced it aloud.

"Oh, some," Julie answered. "Do you?"

"Once in a while," I said, my face flushing. "Anything serious for you?" My heart pounded as I waited for her answer.

"No, not yet. How about you?" she said, her brown eyes twinkling.

I wondered if she sensed my nervousness as I answered in a laughing manner, "Not yet!" When I asked her if it would be okay for me to write her a letter occasionally the look on her face let me know she was pleased with the idea.

At Evangel that fall I spent quite a bit of time in the

prayer chapel, asking God if Julie was the right girl. I let Him know that if Julie was the girl He had chosen for me, it was all right.

Convinced of God's favor, I anxiously awaited my Christmas vacation.

On New Year's Eve, while driving Julie home through the falling snow, I told her that I loved her and why. I also asked her to marry me.

Softly she said, "David, I would like to say yes because I love you too, but first I must pray and make sure it's God's will."

Her answer made me admire her all the more. That was the kind of girl I wanted to marry.

Six weeks later, Julie said yes. We set our wedding date for August 15, the summer after I graduated from Evangel.

I felt as if I were the happiest man in all the world the day I married Julie. Noel was my best man and Coach Landis was there.

As I looked into the radiant face of my beautiful bride, my love for her seemed to know no limits. I knew why I was marrying Julie. Her Christlike character had attracted me. I had watched her live above her circumstances in a very difficult home situation. Julie had worked her way through high school and college. Her zest for life flowed out of her walk with God. Julie knew how to be her own person who could dream dreams and yet believe in mine.

Later we moved to the Chicago area so I could attend Trinity Evangelical Divinity School in Deerfield, Illinois, to prepare for the ministry. The months rolled by as I settled into the academic routine.

Friday, February 12, 1968, began as a very ordinary day. However, it proved to be a day that would drastically change the direction of our lives.

Since Julie had the day off from teaching school, I asked, "Why don't you come to class with me?"

"Good idea," she responded, happy not to have to spend a rainy, dreary day in our little apartment alone— even though it was elegantly furnished with 70 dollars' worth of contemporary Goodwill and modern Salvation Army.

Trinity had a daily chapel service, which we attended that morning. The speaker was a graduate from Columbia Bible College who was ministering in a South American country. The redheaded, middle-aged man made a fiery presentation. He rattled off statistics that showed the world in need. "Nine out of 10 Christian workers stay right here in the United States," he said.

From my seat in the third row I critiqued the exciting message as good seminarians should, but I thought his message was not applicable to me. God had not called me to work overseas, and I knew why: I simply didn't have what it takes.

Why aren't the gifted and talented ones going since the need is so great? I thought. *I'm sure God is calling many who are not answering.*

At the close of his 20-minute message the speaker said, "Every born-again believer should get down on his knees and tell the Lord Jesus Christ he is available to work on foreign soil."

Those words arrested my attention. He continued, "If God doesn't call you, you are no less spiritual."

Relief flooded me as I thought, *Oh, good, because I'm trying to follow the Lord with all my heart.*

I could not conceive of going overseas, especially if it necessitated learning another language. But that speaker's words would not leave my mind.

Every believer, I thought. *How interesting. I've never asked God if I should go or not.*

That evening in our little apartment, I said to Julie, "How can you be a follower of Christ if you aren't willing to do absolutely anything He asks?"

She shrugged as if she knew the answer, but was carefully considering the implications while letting me think about it.

The following morning, we knelt together at the couch and I said, "Lord, I want You to know this morning that we are available to work anywhere in the world for You." In that moment the availability issue was settled, and we never expected any more to come of it. In fact, I thought the whole matter was finished. But over the next few weeks I got the feeling that maybe, just maybe, God was calling us to overseas service.

It can't be from God, I'd tell myself. *It's just me; it's in my mind.*

I was even presumptuous enough to say, "Lord, You can't be talking to me about this because I can't learn another language. I'm making a D in Greek right now."

Later I read in the Bible how Moses explained to God how he couldn't go to Egypt because he was slow of speech. "God, I understand Moses' problem," I said with enthusiasm. However, I made my mistake when I continued to read because I learned God spoke to Moses saying, "Who gave man his mouth? I will help you speak and will teach you what to say."

I knew God was speaking to me through His Word, and I desperately wanted His will for my life, but I felt so inadequate. What if something happened to Julie or she got sick? I was concerned, yet something deep inside of me knew this was only an excuse.

You know I'm first in Julie's life, said that still, small voice. *That was the first reason you were attracted to her.*

How true that was. Knowing there could never be any excuses acceptable to the Lord, I simply said, "Yes, Lord."

A friend gave Julie the book *Hudson Taylor and Maria, Pioneers to China* by John Pollack, and told her she just had to read it. We read it together each night. We were astounded at the Taylors' love and sacrifice for the Chinese people. The more we read, the more we realized the supreme, voluntary sacrifice of Christ for our sins was the motivating factor behind Hudson and Maria's compassion. Deep in our hearts we realized the couple did not just intellectually accept the fact of Christ's sacrifice on the cross; they were fully consumed by it. They clearly saw in the sacrifice of Christ God's own self-giving, compassionate love for people. The Taylors believed the only way to express their gratitude to God was to carry that love to others.

Shouldn't Julie and I be willing to do the same? I thought.

After completing the last chapter, we began to weep in God's presence. Love and concern washed over us in waves and we found ourselves saying, "God, will You please send us to a people with whom we can share the love You have given us?"

We had come full circle from saying, "That's impossible," to, "We're available," to, "Please send us." And indeed we now believed He would do just that, but we didn't know where.

One Sunday afternoon while Julie was dozing in the warm spring sunlight that streamed into our bedroom, I propped myself beside her with a pillow. My self-imposed assignment for the afternoon was to begin reading a huge book entitled *The Worldmark Encyclopedia of Nations*. I'd decided if we were headed to foreign soil, I'd better start studying about the rest of the world. The first country listed in the book was Afghanistan.

The book introduced the country of Afghanistan to me in a nutshell: Islamic nation; landlocked; borders USSR, China, Pakistan, Iran; estimated population 15 million; 25 percent nomadic; 90 percent or more illiterate; nearly 20 spoken languages; Pushtu and Persian (Dari) the dominant languages; few paved highways; no railroads.

A few weeks later one of my seminary classes required an area studies research paper. I chose Central Asia. In my studies I learned about a group of people who at that time numbered more than 10 million. The British called them Pathans (pronounced like batons but beginning with a p). They referred to themselves as Pushtuns (Pushtoons). I was somewhat embarrassed I had never heard of them, for they were the largest tribal group in the world.

Who are these people who continually invade my consciousness? I asked myself.

Further reading revealed they spoke the Pushtu language and lived mostly in Eastern Afghanistan, as well as Pakistan. Many lived in the area of the famous Khyber Pass, which thankfully I had heard of. I further learned they had never been fully subjugated by anyone.

To my fascination I found they lived according to a code of honor called *Pushtunwali*. This stringent code includes *badal* (revenge, which they call "exchange"), *melma-palina* (gracious hospitality), and *nanawati* (the giving of asylum, even to your enemy). The more I read, the clearer it became this was a tough, religious people. They are Muslims who vigorously defend the honor of the Almighty. In some areas they are as rugged as the land they occupy, and rifles, pistols, and knives are a common part of their attire.

Quickly and quietly these brave, tribal people and their harshly beautiful land began to captivate my heart.

As I studied various scholarly books written by both Eastern and Western experts, I began to understand what it meant to be a Muslim. I also gained insight into the sociological structure of Afghanistan and other Islamic societies.

Scholars state that a Muslim's culture, politics, education, religion, and social behavior are woven tightly together. They wrote that being loyal to your family, tribe, and society is not only valued, but demanded. Anyone who wanders too far from the norm is viewed as disloyal, whether living in his own homeland or abroad. Usually such a person is socially and physically ostracized from family and society, and may even be put to death. Why? Because this person is perceived as one who has betrayed, disgraced, dishonored, and shamed his family and people. Outsiders or even those within the society who are considered responsible for causing such a distinct change are often thought of as unscrupulous and dangerous, and they are dealt with accordingly.

Carefully studying authorities on Islamic culture and societies sobered me. I began to attempt to place my feet in the sandals of a Muslim.

In order to conform, I wondered if a Muslim sometimes thought one way in his heart and acted another. I also wondered about his basic human rights—to think freely, to question, and to choose.

Though I did not know all of the answers to my questions, I knew one thing: I was looking forward to the privilege of meeting these people.

More than 11 years had gone by since I had sat in the back pew of Reverend Caldwell's South Carolina church. Nine months had passed since we had heard the man speak in chapel. Now, a summons from Christ sounded that stirred the depths of my soul. I wanted to be near the Pushtuns, to know them. I wanted to laugh when they laughed and to cry when they cried. I wanted my tongue to speak the intricacies of their language and my ears to hear their music. I wanted to be one with them.

Without reservation, God gave me a Pushtun heart.

5

BURST OF JOY

At first our plans were to go to Pakistan, not Afghanistan. It made no difference to Julie and me which side of the border we lived on, as long as we could honor our call to the Pushtun people of Central Asia. After application and acceptance for overseas service by the Assemblies of God, we resigned the church we had founded in Lansing, Illinois, and moved into a small apartment. During this time of preparation I felt a restlessness I could not explain, a feeling we should go to Afghanistan instead of Pakistan.

Why? I wondered. I knew of no reason. Was this just in my mind?

One night, after Julie was asleep, I padded around in my slippers, seeking the Lord for counsel. Exhausted and frustrated, I finally sat down at the kitchen table and said, "God, what are You saying to me?" I heard nothing but the steady hum of the refrigerator. Opening the Old Testament to the Book of Ruth, I read how that newly widowed young woman had followed her mother-in-law Naomi, also widowed, to another country instead of going home to her parents. An illogical and difficult response for this young woman to make, perhaps, but it was prompted by her love for God and her desire to follow His will.

In a way I didn't fully understand, that story said to

me we should go to Afghanistan. I couldn't explain it; I just knew it. Yet my cautious side prompted me to check out this feeling of certainty. So I prayed, "Lord, let Julie select the same book out of the 66 books of the Bible." That would be my test of confirmation—a test made more significant by the fact the Book of Ruth was not normally considered a book of guidance.

"Julie," I said the next morning, "I feel I have confirmation we should go to Afghanistan, but I want to test it to be sure."

"Okay," she said.

"Take the day to read and pray so God can show you," I told her. "Don't worry about anything. I've asked God to lead you today to the same book in the Bible He used to speak to me."

"Okay, I will," she said as she rose from bed and started toward the door to the other room.

She hadn't walked but a few feet when she started humming, "Whither Thou Goest, I Will Go," the popular song based on the story of Ruth. She stopped, furrowing her brow as if she was thinking very hard. I waited for her to speak.

"David, is it the Book of Ruth?" she finally asked.

I sat straight up in bed. She hadn't taken all day to sweat it out as I had; she had taken 90 seconds!

I was strangely perturbed. Seeing my consternation, Julie laughed and said, "Honey, God understood there were other things I needed to get done today."

The weeks and months passed quickly. Julie and I spoke to congregations in many areas of the Midwest. During that time, we also purchased clothes and small appliances that would be packed and later sent in our shipment.

Soon it was time for us to drive to Ohio to spend time with our families and say farewell.

Besides our families, the one other person I had to see before we left was Noel. So I arranged to fly to South Carolina to see him.

Noel's familiar smile greeted me as I stepped off the jet. We exchanged greetings and while we walked to the car he casually remarked, "I suppose you're not hungry."

"No, starved!" I replied enthusiastically.

"Good, Joyce's southern fried chicken is waiting."

Once again it was good to see this humble yet accomplished man. As usual, he conveyed a quiet confidence in God that encouraged me all the more. Noel had earned a master's of science degree from the Massachusetts Institute of Technology. When I went to visit, he was serving as the chairman of the Engineering Technology Division at Midlands Tech in Columbia, South Carolina. He would later earn a doctorate from the University of South Carolina.

Just as promised, red-haired Joyce, looking as lovely as ever, provided chicken with all the trimmings. As we sat down to eat, Noel and Joyce began to bombard me with questions.

In her delightful southern accent, Joyce asked, "Dave, how's Julie? We sure do miss her. It's too bad she couldn't come with you. We would love to see her."

"I wish Julie could have come, and so does she," I answered. "But she needed to spend as much time as possible with her mother. You know her mom has not been in good health since her stroke 13 years ago. It's painful for Julie to have to leave her. But it lessens the pain to know her mother understands our calling from God to serve overseas."

Noel mentioned Julie's father, then asked, "What about his health? What does he think about your going to Afghanistan?"

"He isn't in the best of health either, but he manages okay. Fortunately, he too believes we are doing the right thing—even if we are moving 11,000 miles away," I answered, as I helped myself to more fried okra and black-eyed peas.

"How about Lucy," Joyce asked.

"As you know, Julie's sister Lucy has lived with us since she was 13. In the fall she will be a senior at Evangel College. She believes in what we're doing, but our leaving won't be easy for her or us."

"Please tell us about your dad," Noel said.

"Dad still enjoys his job at Packard Electric," I said. "Right before I came down here we went fishing again in Mosquito Lake. He has a nice boat now. I think he originally thought all this was just talk."

"Well, you do talk a lot," Noel joked.

"Yeah, you're right," I laughed. "But Dad understands and only wants me to do what God wants me to do."

"How about some sweet potatoes, Dave?" Joyce said, smiling as she passed me the plate. As I shook my head, Joyce questioned, "And your mom?"

"You know my mom. She gave me to the Lord the day she knew I was conceived. Mom has never considered me hers; always I have been God's. She'll miss us sure enough, but to her the most important thing is that Julie and I obey the Lord. She's some lady."

Noel took a sip of his sweetened iced tea and said, "You're fortunate your families are so supportive."

I swallowed the last bite of cornbread, reflected on Noel's words for a moment, then responded, "I really think so. You know, Julie and I weren't raised in trouble-free homes. You know the difficulties, tensions, and struggles we had. So it's encouraging to know we go with our parents' blessings. There will be enough challenges facing us in Afghanistan without the heartache of knowing our parents don't understand."

We had left the table and settled in by the fireplace for pecan pie and coffee when Joyce said, "Dave, tell us about some of the adjustments you and Julie will have to make in Afghanistan."

"I know one adjustment we'll have to make," I said with a grin. "We like to hold hands when we walk. In Afghanistan, any display of affection in public is culturally offensive. We'll need to really be careful because we want to be as sensitive to the people as possible."

Noel asked, "Will the Afghan people understand you?"

"I don't know. It's a risk. I just know Christ has placed a deep love in our hearts for them and we have to go."

"But won't people here expect visible, measurable results from your efforts?" Noel continued.

"Maybe, but how do you measure shared love?" I replied. "The purpose of my life is to obey and please God. The results of my obedience are up to Him."

As I flew back to Ohio to rejoin Julie and our folks, memories lingered of all the good days Noel and I had had together over the years. I realized once again God had blessed me with a very special friend.

The last few days with our families were filled with emotion as we said our farewells. Returning to Illinois, we finished our packing and on August 16, 1976, the day after our wedding anniversary, we began the first leg of our flight to Afghanistan on Air France. Several time zones later, we boarded an Iran Air flight that brought us to our final destination.

Our hearts raced as we looked out the jet's window. Like two children peeking through a keyhole, our faces were pressed against the small pane, anxiously waiting to catch our first glimpse of Kabul, Afghanistan's capital and largest city. Our descent offered us a clear view of the surrounding mountains. Their beauty surpassed anything we had seen in pictures.

We're finally here, I thought. God's vision and grace had sustained us throughout all the years of preparation and anticipation. Indeed, in just a few moments our feet would touch the soil of the nation to which God had called us, and we would meet face-to-face the people who did not yet know how much we already loved them.

The aircraft dropped quickly to the landing strip, causing my stomach to lurch. The great tires screeched and the plane taxied to a stop.

"Exciting landing," I remarked.

"Uh-huh," Julie answered.

Disembarking instructions were given in both Persian and English. For the most part, they fell on deaf ears.

As we stepped off the plane into the warm, dry air, Julie and I looked at each other and smiled. I reached out to take her hand, but quickly drew it back and looked around.

When we walked into the barren airport our joy bumped headlong into reality. Other than one day in Mexico and a few days in Canada, Julie and I had never before ventured outside the United States. We had no experience in foreign airports, and there was no one to meet us. In fact, "little" aptly describes how much we knew about most cultural things. We had no idea about such things as money exchange, tipping skycaps, and passport control. In fact, we didn't even know how to ask where the restroom was. Anxiety and frustration dogged me, and the loss of control over my situation made me feel weak and inadequate.

To make matters worse it was Ramadan, the Islamic month of fasting. During this time no one works unnecessarily. Airport workers and passengers cleared out very quickly, leaving the building almost empty.

There we stood in the middle of Kabul's large airport with all of our belongings surrounding us, feeling very lost. To keep from feeling completely overwhelmed, we sat down and whispered a prayer for help.

A skycap, looking rather shabby in his gray coveralls and large billed cap, glanced our way. He must have sensed we were stranded. Our obvious perplexity and confusion must have made him feel sorry for us. He walked over to us, making a lot of hand motions in a sincere effort to communicate meaningfully. But we could not understand what he was trying to say.

At last, he walked behind a nearby counter, opened a drawer, and pulled out a private telephone he placed on the counter. I breathed a little sigh of relief and showered him with thanks in English, which I was sure he did not understand.

I managed to dial correctly the one number I had of a man named Jack McMillan who lived in the city. We had never met this man and I prayed he would be at home.

After a single ring I heard a soft Scottish voice say, "Hello."

I introduced myself and asked him if he could help us.

"Dave," he said, "don't go anyplace. I'll be right over."

"I can assure you, we're not going anywhere," I replied.

In about 20 minutes, Jack arrived. After loading our suitcases and other miscellaneous articles into his little blue car, we were surprised to see there was still enough room for the three of us.

During the trip across town, Julie and I were delighted with our first sights of Kabul. We saw the mud masonry buildings and walls we had read so much about and the sheep and goats meandering along the streets. Most importantly, though, we were able to get our first look at the people.

Jack stopped the car so we could thank God for allowing us to be in this great land. Tears of joy came to our eyes as we thanked Him. After eight years of planning, praying, and preparing, we now had the privilege of actually putting our feet on Afghan soil. I turned to Julie and Jack and smiled. In fact, I found myself smiling at the whole world. But mostly I smiled at God, because He had brought us here.

Jack once again started his car and began making his way toward our destination. Finally we arrived at the home of Jim and Nancy, friends with whom we would be staying. Jim and Nancy had lived near Julie and me in Chicago. The four of us had often dreamed of one day being together in Kabul. Now that day had arrived.

Their house, set back from the street, allowed for a beautiful garden to be planted between several fruit trees. Ripening apples hung from a tree near the whitewashed wall that surrounded the house and garden. Jim and Nancy were surprised to see us because they hadn't received the telegram we had sent announcing our arrival. Laughter, greetings, and hugs were thrown together and engulfed by the chatter of everyone talking at once.

After Jack finally said good-bye, Nancy prepared tea

and cookies while Julie and I rattled on about our trip. A little later, Jim left to make a trip across town. Julie and Nancy started discussing practical matters about living in Kabul, so I slipped away upstairs to a little balcony. I stood by the black iron rail, looking over the part of the city I could see from this vantage point. It felt good to be alone. I needed time to contemplate and absorb the impressions of my surroundings.

The evening panorama of the majestic mountains was more solidly real. It showed a different face of beauty than what I had seen earlier from the air.

I gazed at the walled-in houses and thought about the people who lived in them. A young, barefoot boy dressed in baggy pants and a traditional white shirt that reached his knees hurried along the street below. He was prodding a reluctant black and white milk cow with the stick in his hand. I wondered where his home was and what life looked like to him. *How does he see things? How does he feel about the future?* I thought.

Everything I beheld and felt and heard was strange to me. *Is this culture shock?* I thought. Even as the thought crossed my mind, I knew it wasn't. In spite of the strangeness of it all, I had the persistent feeling I had finally come home, and I knew I was right on time.

Suddenly I wanted to touch, see, feel, taste, and smell absolutely everything I possibly could in this enchanting land. I found myself thinking, *I'm here. I'm here. At last I'm here!* I was like a child at the state fair—ready to ride everything and eat everything at the same time.

Leaning on the rail, I watched the sun drop past the highest mountain peaks, signaling the end of the warm Afghan day. The evening breeze made dust swirl low to the ground, and a stillness blanketed the city.

Suddenly that stillness was shattered by the startling wail of the Islamic call to prayer. Though I had read about this call, I had never experienced it. The cry pierced me deep inside and set me searching for the origin—some minaret hidden from my view. The *mullah's* (priest's) undulating chant dominated the whole area. The stillness of the evening was accentuated when his quivering voice, a familiar part of the call that is unique to the Islamic world, echoed and died between chants.

I knew from my studies the Arabic words were saying, "God is great." The cry from the minaret was calling Muslims to say their prayers.

The call ended as abruptly as it has begun. Silence again engulfed the city as the day fell asleep.

Standing at the doorway of the future, I reflected on the past. I let my mind bathe in the warm realization the persistence of the last eight years was well worth it.

Quietly I began to talk to God. I prayed about the future. I prayed about my sense of inadequacy. I prayed about my thrilling yet fearful anticipation. Then I thanked the Lord for a safe journey, for the nation of Afghanistan, and for its people. My thanksgiving brought new confidence to my heart and I thought, *Lord, I can trust You with our future.*

With that thought lingering in my mind, I reluctantly turned from the balcony and walked softly downstairs.

I lay awake as the night's muffled sounds emerged from my new land. I again whispered thanks for my first day in Afghanistan, knowing I would never forget it.

We stayed with Jim and Nancy for the next two weeks. During that time they helped us become familiar with Kabul by driving us to different areas of the city. Julie and I learned from our hosts that Kabul's population was about

700,000. Its elevation is more than a mile, and mountains ring the city. Summer days can be quite warm, but because of low humidity they're generally comfortable.

We were told the winter's cold temperatures could freeze the water pipes. Although snow usually covered nearby mountains and foothills, the days were generally bright and sunny.

"Nobody has central heat here," Nancy reminded us. Then, laughingly, she said, "So when we do get a freeze, you'll know it."

Snow in Kabul meant work. Every rooftop had to be cleared before the snow melted and ruined its flat mud masonry. Those rooftops and the city's architecture in general fascinated me the most.

During the first few weeks we spent quite a bit of time on foot strolling near Kabul University observing students coming and going from classes and watching people bargain with merchants for goods in the bazaars.

We noticed immediately the Afghan fondness for bright colors. A vast array of colors adorns the Afghans' clothes, homes, and trucks.

Julie was intrigued by their gardening skills. Many homes looked like an oasis with lush gardens, plants, and flowers—a stark contrast to the harsh brown land so typical of Afghanistan's topography.

We didn't grow tired of sightseeing, but we began to feel impatient after a couple of weeks knowing it was time to seriously look for a house to rent.

With all our hearts, we hoped that residence visas would soon be provided. Yet though we waited and waited, the proper visas were not forthcoming.

Before we had enough time to become discouraged, however, we met a young English teacher who was preparing to leave the area. She gave us the name of the owner of the house she was renting, a physician named Dr. Shafe. When we approached him and told him our visa situation, this kind gentleman agreed to let us rent the house on a month-to-month basis. Furthermore, he had the house painted at his own expense before we moved in. Julie and I were grateful for Dr. Shafe's kindness to us, and we prayed for him on many occasions. It was an exciting day for us when we moved into his little house with our few possessions.

About three months after we moved we joyfully received the news we had been granted residence visas.

We felt safe and comfortable among the friendly, open Afghans. Indeed, we were prepared to share our lives with them. Yet we were soon to realize our deep desire was not enough. There was a very difficult barrier separating us. But I was determined to find a way through that wall.

6

SAY IT AGAIN AND AGAIN

The barrier separating us from the Afghans was, of course, our language difference. Anyone who has traveled in a foreign country knows pantomime only goes so far. I could successfully "ask" a merchant where to find face soap through animation, but I could not get an answer when I tried to "ask" how to reach the closest bus stop. I needed to enroll in a language course as soon as possible.

Because I could not find a Pushtu language teacher, I enrolled in a Dari course. About a month later, on the advice of one of my Dari teachers, I went to see Mr. Raheme, a man who could possibly recommend an instructor of Pushtu. While I previewed some Pushtu material, Mr. Raheme phoned a professor from Kabul University named Munsif.

"I'm sorry," Mr. Munsif said, "but my schedule is so busy and you asked me about teaching two weeks ago. Still I am just too busy."

However, at Mr. Raheme's insistence Mr. Munsif agreed to meet with us a few days later.

Mr. Munsif's arrival at Mr. Raheme's office turned out to be one of those important moments in life that slip in quietly. In fact, they are moments that often go totally unnoticed. Unobtrusively he was just there.

Mr. Munsif was a thin man with a sharp nose and distinct features. Neatly dressed in a tan suit, his tall, straight appearance gave him a good bearing. He appeared to be in his late thirties.

As we talked, I knew this Afghan gentleman had an unexplainable concern for Julie and me—two strangers who had come to his land. Because of what he had said to Mr. Raheme, I was very surprised when Mr. Munsif agreed to teach us. Our two-hour lessons would be held each afternoon in his office after he finished teaching at the university.

Why Mr. Munsif agreed to teach us was a puzzle. *Maybe he sees something like family in us,* I thought. *Or maybe it's our sincere desire to learn his Pushtu language. More than likely it is just because of his kindness.*

Looking back on Mr. Munsif's decision, I now know it was more than any of those reasons. He agreed because God was working things out for the best for all of us.

Mr. Munsif was, indeed, a very remarkable man. He was a leader in his tribe in southeastern Afghanistan, as was his father. His family had considerable landholdings.

While other university professors may have been trustworthy and had teaching ability as well, there was only one Mr. Munsif. He truly was an Eastern man who could understand a Western mind. That was a very good trait, because there was only one David Leatherberry enrolled in Pushtu language studies.

It took me six months just to learn how to differentiate and repeat the Pushtu sounds. Yet day after day Mr. Munsif's patience with me never wavered. He seemed honored that I wanted to learn Pushtu. Thus he was always encouraging me. Never once did he speak a single word in anger, nor did he become frustrated by how slowly I was learning his language.

Though I studied hard and repeated each word carefully, my efforts to learn how to speak Pushtu seemed to drag on and on. In fact, I was convinced I had to be the worst Pushtu student in the long history of the language.

Mr. Munsif and I became good friends. This did not happen because he could practice English with me or that I offered some advantage by being a foreigner. Our friendship grew simply because he liked me and I liked him.

Shortly after Mr. Munsif became our teacher, he and I went for a walk around our neighborhood, listening to the Pushtu shopkeepers. He did this to help me learn the language.

In one particular shop Mr. Munsif spoke with a young man who was about 15 years old. Then Mr. Munsif spent several minutes talking with other members of the family.

When we stepped outside once again, Mr. Munsif said, "This young man, Ajmal Masoude, speaks beautiful Pushtu. His family has given you permission to come into the shop and practice your language studies anytime."

"Thank you," I said. Yet all the while I was thinking, *That fellow Ajmal doesn't realize how patient he will have to be.*

The shop, owned by Ajmal's eldest brother, Rahman, was filled with miscellaneous items. It was sort of an Afghan version of the five-and-dime. Ajmal helped Rahman and his other brother Khadim stock and sell soap, gum, and other odds and ends. His was a close family that practiced good moral principles and gave generously to the poor.

Mr. Masoude never allowed Ajmal to take even the smallest payment for helping us with our language studies. Though I assisted Ajmal with the English lessons he was taking, my help was small compared to the help he gave to Julie and me.

I felt indebted to Ajmal's father because he later allowed his son to come to our house for language practice. On several occasions, Ajmal arrived bearing gifts from his mother—mainly special Afghan dishes she had prepared.

Sometimes Ajmal's father invited me to their home. There he, his three sons, and I enjoyed delicious Afghan meals. Never once, however, did I see his daughters or his wife who prepared those tasty dishes. That was culturally forbidden.

Julie was delighted when the Masoudes invited both of us to dinner for the first time. As soon as we arrived, Julie was escorted to a room with the women and I joined the men in another room in true Afghan style.

I had been studying Pushtu with Ajmal for about five months when we invited his family to go with us on a picnic. Mr. Masoude accepted "with pleasure."

Because this would be the first time we would be with the entire family, Julie spent several days planning the menu for that special event.

As she prepared the final grocery list she said, "David, I hope they'll like what I am going to fix." I told her not to worry because I felt certain the family would enjoy what Julie made.

When the appointed day finally arrived, Ajmal's mother became ill and could not go on the outing. With remorse, she sent her regrets to us. Julie was disappointed, but she felt strongly that since Mrs. Masoude could not attend the picnic, she should not go either. We later learned that Julie's decision was the culturally polite and correct thing to do, and that Ajmal's mother was touched by her sensitivity.

I began to prepare for the three-hour trip to the picnic spot by concentrating on a few Pushtu words and a couple of short sentences. Because Ajmal's father and brothers knew no English, I wanted to be able to say a few things to them in their own language. Yet despite my preparation, I could not initiate a single proper sentence in Pushtu during the entire trip. Though I listened carefully and tried desperately to remember words, in the end I had to rely on Ajmal to translate what I said in English.

It seemed unreal I could neither initiate nor properly respond in Pushtu after my many weeks of study. This inability made me feel terrible. How I cared about these friends and wanted to communicate with them in their own tongue. Yet in spite of my language deficiencies, we enjoyed the trip and the fine meal we had when we reached the scenic garden park in Jalalabad.

It was late when I arrived home that evening, and Julie had already gone to bed. It was just as well. My disappointment over my lack of ability to communicate with the Masoudes in Pushtu was so overwhelming, I didn't want to talk to anyone—not even to Julie.

Kneeling and weeping, I cried out, "Lord, I couldn't get one word right—not one word! I feel such love for Ajmal and his family, yet I can hardly express myself at all. Lord Jesus, I want to give myself, my life to the Pushtuns, but how can I ever express Your love to them if I can't even learn their language?"

At that moment, these words came suddenly and forcibly to my consciousness. *David, I used David Wilkerson to open the hearts of those teenage gangs in New York City, didn't I? Can't I use you to show my love to the Pushtuns?*

I thought, *David Wilkerson, whose book,* The Cross

and the Switchblade, *I had read so many times? Here I am struggling because I can say precious little in the Pushtu language and God brings that thought to my mind? What did this mean? Maybe God is saying that He can use any man who is open to be used—even me.*

Indeed I knew God had opened an effective door of ministry to people He cared about through the ministry of David Wilkerson. Dared I believe perhaps God could use me among the Afghans? With thanksgiving I received that thought from the Lord. My discouragement disappeared and I knew I would not quit trying to learn Pushtu.

In the spring of 1977 I enrolled at Kabul University for additional language study. Taking the university courses and continuing private study with Mr. Munsif was extremely taxing for me. By August, I was ready for a break. That particular break would become one of the most adventuresome and unique excursions of my life.

7

TREK IN THE HINDU KUSH

The region where northeast Afghanistan meets Tajiki-
stan, Pakistan, and China is called the Pamir Knot. This
incredible collection of lofty mountain peaks is often
referred to as the "roof of the world." Many of its peaks
rise above 20,000 feet. This area attracts numerous international mountain climbers every year.

Flowing out of the Pamir Knot is the historic, 600-mile-
long Hindu Kush Range, which forms the backbone of
Afghanistan. This range seems to express the very soul of
the country. In fact, some have said that it is Afghanistan.

Julie and I had been so absorbed in language study
during our first year in Afghanistan, we were not fully
aware of the Hindu Kush and its impact on Afghan life.
Therefore, we were delighted when our friends Joe and
Dawn Miller, teachers at an international school in Kabul,
obtained a government permit and invited us to join them
and five other friends on a hike in the Hindu Kush. The
others were Tom Larson, a sturdily built American student visiting for the summer; Ole Peterson, my Swedish
classmate at Kabul University; Olga Swenson from Swe-
den and Betty Ann Jones from England, who were nurses
living in Kabul; and Bernice Whatley, a school administra-
tor.

Experienced hikers told us the trip would be very strenuous. Thus we began to get in shape by doing calisthenics and taking short hikes up and down the historic Kabul wall—an ancient wall built between two low-lying mountains for protection from foreign invaders.

My excitement about the trip was tinged with concern because my doctor had told me in 1971 I should not go overseas due to my lung condition. Furthermore, cold temperatures, especially at high altitudes, could create a serious problem for me. However, I desperately wanted to be part of the hiking team and I believed with training and God's help I could participate.

Our adventure began on August 18 with a trip in two four-wheel-drive vehicles—a jeep and a Land Rover. On a paved road, we drove north from Kabul to the city of Khanabad, then proceeded on a dirt road to a desolate place called Kislem. There we pitched our tents in a field for the night.

At 2 a.m. we awoke to the shouts of Bob and Dawn: "There's water! There's water everywhere!"

Stumbling around in the darkness, we grabbed our possessions and fled to higher ground.

The landowner who had given us permission to stay there had neglected to mention the field would be irrigated that night.

Later that morning I awoke with a start to the sound of high-pitched voices and jingling bells. "More water?" I asked, peering out of our tent.

Shading my eyes from the bright sun, I saw several nomadic Pushtun families with their sheep, goats, and camels parading by. Colorfully dressed women sat atop the swaying, humped beasts that were led along by their halters. Chattering children and barking dogs darted in and out among them as they made their way past us. It was a beautiful sight.

Later that morning we left Kislem and headed toward Faizabad, a town only about 50 miles from the Soviet border. For part of the trip we were on a treacherous mountain road that at times clung to a narrow strip of space carved from sheer cliffs. At other times the road dipped sharply to cross dry riverbeds. Often the rise was so steep we could not see the road.

The white Land Rover Julie and I were in clawed its way up the inclines like a frightened cat, sliding and spitting stones as it slowly moved forward. We hung on tightly and leaned toward the mountain, hoping our twisting vehicle would not hit a rock, lose its balance, and, with a lurch, throw us down the mountain into the deep river below.

After a night in Faizabad we arrived the next day at the village of Fargzhamu. That was where our hike would begin.

Around our campfire in Fargzhamu, we prayed for Julie who was sick with fever and diarrhea. We also prayed God would give us a safe journey. All of us were powerfully reminded we could put our trust and security in the Lord. The next morning Julie was well.

We bought two pack donkeys from the local people. Since the villagers realized none of us knew anything about handling pack animals, much less purchasing them, they tried to sell us three donkeys. However, we were convinced they were trying to take advantage of naive foreigners, so we opted to only buy two. The donkeys would carry all of the gear and medicine we needed for our journey. In addition, each team member would carry a backpack of 25 to 40 pounds. Loading the donkeys, we set out along the Kowkcha River on a rocky narrow path.

During our second day on the high trail we made some insightful discoveries about donkeys. It is true they are sturdy and sure-footed beasts. They are also just the right size for picking their way along very narrow ledges while bearing quite heavy loads. However, if a donkey's load is too heavy or loaded improperly, the animal wobbles. It wasn't long before we also noted that as they strain to carry their burdens, tears run down their sad-looking faces.

At first we loaded the two animals improperly—not high enough up on their backs. They responded by not going forward at all. The only way to solve the problem was to take off half their load, lead them up the mountain and unload that gear, then take them back down the mountain for the other half of the load. Loaded once again, we had to march them over the same terrain to reach the level where we had left the first half of our gear. This time-consuming, backbreaking procedure made twice as much work for the animals and four times the labor for us. In short, we did need three donkeys. "Those villagers were smarter than we thought," we mumbled to ourselves.

While we were going through the donkey procedure, Julie told me she wanted to walk on ahead. I watched as she trudged up the mountain. She was dressed in blue jeans, a long green tunic top, brown hiking boots, and a big, wide-brimmed white hat that was being tugged at by the wind. She bobbed along confidently, finally disappearing from my view as she went over the ridge.

I had only turned back to my task for a few moments when I thought I heard Julie's voice of alarm. I cocked my head to listen. Since Julie is a self-sufficient woman who doesn't usually panic, I knew she would not call unless she was in serious trouble. I thought perhaps the wind was playing tricks on me. Yet as I listened closely, I heard her call again.

I sprinted up the narrow trail and over the ridge to find Julie flattened against the rocky face of the mountain like putty on plate glass. She had missed the main trail, and the deceptive sand and gravel path she had chosen had shifted beneath her feet. In a split second, she had plastered herself against the face of the rock far beyond my reach. She had nothing to hold on to, neither did she have a foothold. How she managed to stay in place, I did not know. We both realized if Julie lost control, she would slide hundreds of feet down the mountain into the rushing river below.

"Don't move!" I said, trying to be calm and not frighten her more. I turned and yelled back to the others, "Come here! Hurry! Julie's in trouble!"

Tom, Ole, Betty, and I grasped hands, forming a human chain. Slowly and carefully we began to creep step by step along the face of the rock. Tom anchored himself firmly on the path as I edged myself in a painfully slow fashion toward Julie. We all knew at any moment we could tumble to our deaths.

When I got close to her, Julie quietly said, "If you take my pack, then I think I can make it."

"Oh, no," I answered quickly, trying to keep panic out of my voice.

Very carefully I reached out, grasped her belt, and we inched our way back toward firm ground. A few feet from safety, somebody's foot slipped, sending some sand and loose rocks tumbling and clattering down the mountain to the river.

"Don't move!" I yelled, my voice echoing off the mountain walls.

Everyone froze. When I knew for certain it would be okay for us to continue, I said, "Slowly now."

Again we began to slide along and grasp the cold stone face. After several agonizing steps, we finally reached safety.

I hugged Julie close and gave a sigh. With deep gratitude I whispered, "Thank You, God. Thank You. Thank You."

Slowly I permitted my adrenaline-charged, perspiring body to sink, trembling, to the ground. I took Julie's hand, almost afraid to let her go even though the nightmare was over. After sitting quietly by me for a few moments, tears of relief trickled down her cheeks.

Concerned about the released tension, someone said, "Watch her for shock."

"Don't worry; the Lord's near me," Julie responded. "Out there I kept calm as I thought over and over what God's Spirit had impressed upon us two nights ago, 'I will be your guard and I will be with you.'"

As we continued our travels, we were thankful we were all safe. With that experience, however, we had gained a greater appreciation for the rugged Hindu Kush and the treacheries hidden beneath her beauty.

On day three we purchased our third donkey. We named this one Harry. Regrettably, Harry proved to be too small to carry our provisions, so the next day we traded him for a handsome gray donkey we called Denny. Unlike our first two donkeys—a likable delinquent and a deserter, once loaded—frisky Denny ran off whenever the other donkeys came into view. Yet in spite of their idiosyncrasies, we came to appreciate Asko, Charlie, and Denny, our three hardworking little animals.

The initial days of our hiking seemed filled with calamities, muscle soreness, learning how to manage the donkeys, and setting up or breaking camp. Hiking in Afghanistan's mountains was more demanding than Julie or I had imagined. On the other hand, the moments of rare beauty also proved to be beyond our imaginations.

Even with three donkeys we were still having trouble transporting our gear, so I purchased Arthur, a larger donkey with a heavy steel halter chain and special shoes on his back hooves. I was willing to pay the high asking price because we were tired of hauling supplies and I wanted a big donkey.

It seemed everyone we met knew Arthur, and in the next village the people challenged me to let him fight.

"Fight?" I asked aloud, all the while thinking to myself, *So that's what the special shoes are for.*

This was a popular betting game in the region. One man brought his choice animal, leading the donkey by his halter just as Americans lead their show horses. Then the men insisted I bring Arthur to fight at the village green. I steadfastly refused, however, which did not endear me to the owner of the other competitor.

Each day on the trail was different from the one before. On one occasion Dawn's life was endangered as she crossed a placid-looking stream that was deeper than it appeared. The stream began to flow with such force she had to cling to an overhanging branch to keep from being swept away.

Another time, I became ill after eating a bad egg we had purchased from some villagers. Because I was too sick to walk, we had to rent a horse, and I was forced to jostle along on its back. Those incidents provided plenty of opportunity for conversation and fellowship among our group, and we traveled together as though we had been friends for many years.

In many special ways, each of the hikers demonstrated God's love to the villagers we met. Because Olga and Betty were nurses, their acts of compassion were the most visible. As we acquainted ourselves with villagers along the trail, Olga and Betty dispensed medicines for eyes, pain, and various kinds of infections. These rural people were in great need of medical help.

In the village of Rabat, Olga and Betty were unable to treat a woman who they thought had tuberculosis of the spine, so we all prayed for her.

One morning a young boy was brought to us. We could see he was in great pain, apparently suffering from appendicitis. Medically our nurses could do very little since they could not perform surgery. While the boy's bearded father tenderly held him in his arms, I knelt beside them both and prayed. My heart ached for this elderly man and his young son.

On the 10th day of our journey, we still had more than a third of the trail to complete. We hired a guide with his donkey to lead us over the cold and windy 13,000-foot Anjoman Pass. At noon we arrived at a high plateau just before our final ascent to the pass.

Upon seeing the beautiful, deep blue, crystal clear Anjoman Lake, Julie exclaimed, "Let's have our lunch here."

There was not a single objection, and we enjoyed the beauty as we ate our food.

Our entourage now included the beautiful black Arabian horse I had ridden when I was ill and a total of five donkeys. Even so, we made good time as we approached the pass. We camped overnight on the trail at an *aylock*—a sheepfold—that was built from stones and protected us from the wind.

But the night's events turned ominous.

Tom, who had stayed behind to catch some fish from Anjoman Lake, became lost and wandered around the mountain for more than six hours. In his attempt to find us, he climbed nearly 2,000 feet higher. With only his light clothes to protect him from the night's bitter cold, he could have frozen to death had he not spotted our camp light. We welcomed him back at about 10:30.

Just as we snuggled down in our sleeping bags, a gun-shot broke the stillness of the night. We never learned the reason for it or the source of the murderous sound, but it was frightening.

Julie and I were glad when daylight finally arrived.

Everyone's nerves were still a bit frayed the next morn-ing, but a peace settled over us as we crossed the crest of the pass. Below us appeared the Panjshir Valley. It was one of the most spectacular views I had ever seen. A river wove its way through the middle of the valley, and on both sides of its banks stood squares of golden grain. Lush fields of beautiful green trees were scattered on the mountain slope.

Excited by what I saw, I exclaimed, "Julie, I'm glad we came, aren't you?"

"Yeah, this is magnificent," she answered.

On the last day of our hike, we walked until darkness overtook us. We had no place to camp that night. We met Basir, a middle-aged fisherman, when hiking about a mile outside his village, Dashti Rawat. Basir invited us to sleep at his home and we eagerly accepted. Once at his home, we spread our sleeping bags on the freshly strawed ground of a walled-in area used by his sheep, goats, and chickens.

For dinner we were treated to a simple but fine meal of fish Basir had caught earlier in the day. We retired with the chickens nesting nearby and slept soundly. That was our last night in the Hindu Kush.

Blinding sunlight awoke me the next morning. *If only I'd crawled further into the sleeping bag*, I thought.

A strange weight on my head and the sounds of farm animals disoriented me. Without moving, I called to Julie. Chuckling, she motioned for my nearby companions to look at me. They laughed when they saw that a chicken was roosting on my head.

Our challenging task that day was to sell the donkeys in the bazaar. As Joe, Tom, Ole, and I started the bargaining, we quickly realized how unprofitable the donkey-trading business is—particularly for foreigners trekking the Hindu Kush. At the beginning of our journey, the villagers knew how much we needed donkeys. At the end, they knew how much we didn't need the animals. After a full day's bargaining, we had to sheepishly admit to the women in our group we had sold the donkeys for only about a third their original cost.

On the bus back to Kabul, Julie and I reminisced and savored the highlights of the past 21 days in the mountains.

Physically I felt better than I had since my high school track days. I had had no trouble with my lung.

Spiritually, the time spent with godly people who prayed and worked together greatly refreshed me. We had ministered to suffering people along the way and talked about God with villagers. I felt victorious.

Our strenuous, exhilarating vacation revitalized me.

Returning to the university, I once again pursued Pushtu with vigor. This turned out to be well-placed vigor because Pushtu had not become any easier while I was gone. Little did I know the man who would continue to help me in my language studies would become one of the most meaningful persons in my life.

8

TRUSTED TEACHER

I brushed my teeth to the rhythm of Pushtu emanating from my tape recorder. I wore a headset around the house, repeating aloud the sentences. At night I was lulled to sleep by the Pushtu equivalent of "apple, apple, banana, banana" and a string of other fruits.

A notebook of phonetics and grammar rules was my constant companion, as were vocabulary and short sentence cards. So constant was my study of Pushtu that on my walks, if I wasn't careful I'd trip over things as I read my words. For the same reason, bike riding became not so much an event as an adventure.

One day I spotted a stalk of ripe bananas hanging outside a small shop. I thought to myself, *Here's my chance to use some words I have learned. I remember banana from the tape last night.* With a sense of adventure and excitement, I stepped under the canopy and exchanged the usual greetings with the shopkeeper, "God's peace be upon you."

"And upon you also," he replied.

"Are you in good health?" I asked.

"I am, thanks. And you?"

"I'm fine."

Finally, after the long exchange of greetings that I knew so well, I bravely said, "*Staw du zarl kala pu tso da?*" I thought that I was asking, "How much are your yellow bananas?" But the perplexed look on the shopkeeper's face made me realize I must not have been clear.

I had made a firm rule for myself: Do not point. Use the word, for you cannot learn the language by pointing. So I repeated the Pushtu sentence a little louder.

He looked straight at me and just shook his head.

Two dirty-faced boys over to my left started giggling. The shopkeeper looked to one side trying to contain his own temptation to laugh.

Turning away to hide my red face, I mumbled, "Thank you. Good-bye."

Quickly, I melted into the crowd on the street.

On my way home from the market, I thought about my track experience at Howland High School. "I did not quit then and I will not quit now," I muttered softly. Then it had been a physical race; now it was a struggle with Pushtu, and I was determined to win.

For about six weeks I struggled through my second course in conversational Pushtu at the university. My professor, Dr. Malgari, was very patient with me, but she had a very professional manner with a no-nonsense approach. When she announced a future assignment would be an oral quiz, I studied diligently. My goal was to at least pass.

On the day of the quiz, I arrived 20 minutes early and sat in one of the desk chairs for a final review. Ole, the bright young Swedish linguist I had hiked with, and a Japanese student came in just before the period started. When Dr. Malgari entered, the three of us rose in the Eastern custom. She exchanged Pushtu greetings with us and then we sat together directly in front of her.

She began with me. With a thin smile she addressed me in Pushtu, using the Arabic translation of my name.

"Good afternoon, Daoud."

"Good day, Dr. Malgari."

"What time did you get up this morning?" she quizzed.

I stared at her, my mind racing. She repeated the question. I sat there acutely aware that my classmates were watching, but still I was unable to comprehend what she said.

"Can you tell me where you live?"

A child's question, but at least I understood. *Carte Char, but how do I phrase the sentence?* I thought to myself. *Oh, please remember.* I lowered my head and thought hard. Then I sighed, raised my head again, and, feeling my cheeks flush, stammered, "Carte Char."

The single-word answer brought a smile of hope to her face. She looked at her notes for the next question.

"Did you have lunch, Daoud?"

Silence.

Twice she repeated it before I said, "*Ho*" (yes).

I wiped perspiration from my palms. I wanted desperately to say to her that I had studied as hard as I could.

"What did you have to eat?" she asked.

By now, I was so flustered I couldn't even remember lunch, let alone the Pushtu names for soup or salad.

"Can you describe this building, Daoud?" she queried once again. Then seeing my red perspiring face and trembling hands, she mercifully cut the exam short saying, "It's okay. We'll try again another time."

Why? Why? Why? I thought. Extremely frustrated, I wanted to scream or cry or something. My deepest desire was to be able to communicate with Afghans in their own tongue, so why were my memory and performance so bad?

When the other students' quizzes ended, we rose to our

feet as the teacher left. Finally free to go, I trudged out of the room.

On the steps in front of the university, discouragement took the spirit out of me. I paused to look at the students crisscross in front of me. Each was intent on his or her destination. Some walked along the cement walkway reading books; others talked with friends who were leaning against the building.

I sighed deeply and thought, *They are all better students than I, no doubt.* Then I whispered, "God, do You see these students here? Do You see the love I have in my heart for Afghans?" In anguish I cried softly, "How will I ever be able to communicate Your love to them?"

Soft words flowed through my mind, *Do you really love these students?*

Well, Lord, You know I do.

Do you truly love them?

"God, You know I do," I mumbled half out loud.

In my mind I thought I was beginning to sound a little like the apostle Peter in his conversation with Jesus on the Galilean beach 2,000 years ago.

Do you love them enough to keep banging your head against this language that is like a brick wall to you, or to persist when you seem to go in a circle? Do you love them enough not to quit?

Before I could answer, my classmate Ole, who was fluent in five languages, walked up beside me. Knowing I had done poorly on the test, he said, "David, you probably think you aren't a very good witness of God's love because you're not doing well in the language, or that you're not making the right impression on people. In reality, the teachers marvel at you. They can't understand what it is that makes you keep coming back when most anyone else would have quit by now. They wonder what motivates you like that."

He put a hand on my shoulder and added a further encouraging word, "Do you know why God gave me a mind for languages and not you?" Answering his own question, Ole said, "Because God knows I'd never have the patience you have to stay with it. You'll learn it, Dave; you'll learn it."

"Thank you, Ole," I said. "I feel a little down just now, but with God's help I'll hang in there."

"Good," he said smiling. "I'll pray for you."

Ole's encouraging words stayed with me as I continued in Kabul University's language program for foreigners. To complete the program, a reading course was required each semester. I found that learning to read simple Pushtu in the strange Arabic script was extremely difficult. My motivation was high, but I progressed slowly. However, in spite of my snail's pace, I felt a deepening desire to read the New Testament in Pushtu. Given my ability, it seemed foolish to attempt this feat until I became a better reader, but I decided I should try it anyway.

Mr. Munsif, my private teacher, was the only one I felt I could possibly approach about my new project. I spent several weeks praying about this matter because I wanted to be careful not to offend him or make him feel that I was taking advantage of our friendship.

In our living room one fall evening after our lesson, Mr. Munsif and I enjoyed a quiet chat as we munched nuts and raisins between sips of tea. Seated in the rosewood armchair across the room from Julie and me, this man lent dignity to our rather plain surroundings. The sun sank from sight in the west and the room's shadows were softened by the warm glow of the lamp. I decided this was the time to speak to him.

Choosing my words carefully, I expressed my long-held desire to read the Bible in Pushtu. Finally, I came to the point and asked him to teach us to read.

Signs of strong feelings I could not interpret flashed across the face of my disciplined, emotionally controlled friend. I watched his dark eyes. For a split second I was afraid I had overstepped an unwritten boundary and had put our special friendship in jeopardy.

"Well, David, do you have that Book in your house?"

"Yes, I do."

He fought to master his emotions. Twice he tried to speak. Then he carefully said, "David, for over two years I have been looking for the Holy Bible in my language so I could read it."

I was so amazed at his words I couldn't speak. Time had stopped. Looking back, I would travel around the world again for that single sacred moment—a moment when the warm friendship we had forged had the feeling of destiny.

Carefully he formed his answer to my question. "Of course, David, I would be pleased to teach you to read it."

The last two months of 1977 passed quickly as I continued my studies with Mr. Munsif. Since the university is closed during January and February, Julie and I decided to spend six of those eight weeks in Jalalabad, a Pushtun city located three hours east of Kabul and about an hour from the famous Khyber Pass. We wanted to do this so we could intensively study the Pushtu language since the primary language of Kabul is Dari.

The difference between the weather in Kabul and Jalalabad in winter is like the difference between Chicago and West Palm Beach, Florida. Surrounded by mountains, Kabul's elevation is about 6,000 feet, whereas Jalalabad's elevation is close to 2,000 feet making it an ideal warm winter retreat.

After deciding to spend time in Jalalabad, Julie and I found out Mr. Munsif's new job temporarily assigned him there for about the same period of time. The three of us were happy about this opportunity to keep studying without interruption.

Mr. Munsif had a friend who owned a beautiful, walled-in garden in Jalalabad. Several enclosed rooms were attached to the wall. His friend graciously offered Julie and me the use of one room and Mr. Munsif the use of another. For this we were very thankful.

During those sunny days in Jalalabad, Mr. Munsif and I spent most of our leisure time together over cups of tea, sharing life experiences. He gradually confided in me that he had made some powerful enemies over the years. While he was at the university, an influential family had tried to pressure him into changing their son's grade. Mr. Munsif refused to compromise his integrity. False charges were brought against him and he was dismissed from that prestigious institution. Not satisfied with his dismissal, the family still harbored resentment and sought further revenge.

Over the weeks, as I listened to Mr. Munsif's views, it occurred to me his love for his country's cherished freedom and the independent spirit of his people may have made political enemies for him as well. One day the thought struck me that his enemies could try to exploit his relationship with me, since I was a foreigner. Foreigners, often wrongly accused of being political agents, brought suspicion on anyone associated with them. The possibility my motives, based on love, might be so grotesquely twisted both chilled and angered me. A troubling storm blew restlessness into my mind and made me unable to sleep. I decided, after thoughtful prayer, I had to speak forthrightly about this matter with my friend.

I wanted to talk with him privately, so we trudged up a hill overlooking the sun-splashed city. We began to share personal feelings, taking on a level of vulnerability only found in the security of true friends.

I began by saying, "You know how much Julie and I both care for you, Mr. Munsif, but our friendship could possibly cause a problem for you and your family. Anytime you feel my relationship is endangering your family or causing hardship in any way, you don't have to say anything. You just don't have to see Julie and me again. I will completely understand."

He smiled, then looked at me for a moment before answering. "I appreciate that, David. If there ever is a point I feel we should not be together, I will take what you've said to heart."

I then told him of my background and how I felt God had directed Julie and me to Afghanistan. I shared with him that I had studied the *Injil* (New Testament) in Greek and the Old Testament in Hebrew.

"You have actually studied the Holy Book in the original languages?" he asked somewhat incredulously.

"Yes, I have," I answered.

I referred again to our being led by God to his country. For Mr. Munsif, the concept of personal, divine guidance was unfamiliar. I tried to explain how one could be led by God's Spirit—that He had spoken to people, such as Moses and Peter, telling them what to do. From our conversations, I knew Mr. Munsif was like Cornelius in the Book of Acts—a God-conscious man who prayed faithfully and was hungry to know the God he talked about continually.

Our time together was good—moments made sacred by a sense of God's presence and marked by great trusting and openness friends savor for a lifetime. I left the hill knowing God had been with me in a very special way. I also knew He had brought two men from contrasting worlds closer to each other for His purpose. I had the distinct feeling I had met a unique man whom God had allowed into my life to make me better for the knowing. Silently I vowed I would work hard to be worthy of that trust.

Before I knew it, the delightful days in Jalalabad ended. Too quickly it was time for us to return to Kabul for me to begin my third semester of language study at the university.

9

THE FOURTH BROTHER

In the days following the April 1978 coup, Julie and I were surprised we were able to remain in the country under the new communist regime. The new government did not invalidate our visas. This meant I could finish my Pushtu program at the university. But should I?

The fearful dilemma Julie and I had discussed after our jeep ride with Chuck was now upon us. We knew a decision had to be made quickly.

To openly or even privately associate with our Afghan friends could jeopardize their lives, since the government now considered us to be imperialistic Americans. On the other hand, we had no desire to abandon our friends who faced all of the dangers brought about by the coup and the subsequent changes in Afghan life.

What should we do?

After much soul-searching and prayer, we knew we should remain in Afghanistan as long as possible. We had the assurance the Holy Spirit would give us wisdom and discernment. I continued my studies at the university.

Although my professors showed the same respect toward me, their faces reflected the stress of the political situation. I'm sure they had to fight off the fear of possibly being punished because of their association with me.

They were guarded in their relationship with me in the classroom and were careful not to express open friendliness toward me on campus. I felt sorry for them, but was thankful for their bravery in continuing to teach me under difficult circumstances.

I awoke one morning in May with my thoughts full of questions. *Would aliens like us be asked to leave, or would our visas simply be canceled? Would there be more fighting? Could I continue my language study?*

Julie and I knew if we had to leave suddenly there would be no time to say good-bye to our friends. Therefore we decided we should go ahead and give our friends the farewell gifts we wanted them to have. If we were allowed to stay longer, so be it. We knew they would understand our actions.

That afternoon Julie and I began our farewell tour, stopping first at the Masoudes' shop. When everyone else had left the small shop, all three brothers were ready to tell us their good news: They had received word from their brother-in-law in the army and he was safe. We rejoiced with them.

I continued to visit quietly with the men while Julie moved over to the umbrella display. She opened an umbrella and held it in front of her as though she was considering purchasing it. She was blocking the view through the window from any prying eyes. Quickly I slipped the gift from Julie's shopping basket into the hands of Ajmal. In an instant, it disappeared under the counter.

Looking directly at Ajmal, I said, "Since we don't know when we might have to leave, we want to give you the most precious gift we can. It is the *Injil* (New Testament). Please present this to your father as a special gift from us to your family."

There was a brief silence before Rahman reached over the counter and shook my hand warmly with both of his. He smiled broadly, as he touched the Book.

Ajmal and Khadim, having seen the exchange, said, "Thank you. Thank you. You have honored our family."

They acted as though we would see them again, yet we all knew this might be our last visit before we were forced to leave their country.

Before it became awkward, we said our good-byes and left. We continued to visit as many of our friends as possible that day, giving each our farewell gift. Returning home late, we breathed a sigh of relief.

During our visits Julie and I had assured our Afghan friends we understood if they were unable to have further contact with us. From that day forward, we went to an Afghan home only if we were invited. When they did extend an invitation, it humbled me to see the risks these loyal friends took.

Tense months marched by. In December 1978 I completed my Pushtu program at Kabul University. In January 1979 our visas expired. During the second week in January, the last week of our stay in Kabul, Mr. Munsif had us over for a farewell meal with his family.

On the appointed day, we took a taxi to Mr. Munsif's home. The entire family was present and they warmly welcomed Julie and me. Emotions were high on this special visit.

Late in the afternoon, shortly before we had to leave, I told Mr. Munsif about my high school track experience. He listened attentively. Then I said, "Mr. Munsif, as a token of our friendship, I want to give you one of my most treasured possessions." As I was speaking, I reached into my bag and handed him my track trophy.

Mr. Munsif looked at the runner, read the championship inscription, then turned his head away from me to absorb a portion of that triumphant moment I'd had. "Thank you, David," he said quietly, holding my strange gift.

Near the end of the week Ajmal's family invited us over for a farewell meal. In recent months we had become so close to them that Julie and I were treated as a son and daughter. Except for Mrs. Masoude's closest male relatives, I was the only other male who had ever been allowed to see her unveiled face since her late childhood.

Upon our arrival at their house, we were ushered into the room reserved only for family members. We sat down on the floor cushions and enjoyed a delicious meal as we recalled our many good times together. As the time for us to leave drew close, they confided in us about some difficulties they faced, so I asked for permission to pray with them. They kindly said yes.

In the seconds before I was to pray, I sensed a special instruction from God: *Explain to them that this time you will pray for them in a special language.*

Wait a minute, Lord, I thought. *You mean I'm to pray in my prayer language with people who probably never heard of such a thing?*

I tried to push the disconcerting thought out of my mind, but it wouldn't go.

I looked around at the patiently waiting family, then I told Ajmal that I would like for him to explain something to his family before I prayed. Using both Pushtu and English, I shared with him what to relate. He carefully explained to them in Pushtu that this gift spoken about in the Holy Bible was a language from God I had never learned. I watched for any feedback. They just nodded and smiled as though he had said nothing unusual. Ajmal continued by telling his family that I would be praying what God wanted me to pray. He explained that I found praying in this manner helped me to pray for needs when I did not know how, even in my mother tongue. He related that this gift language helped me worship God, for I could say all the beautiful things in my heart I could not otherwise express to God.

Throughout Ajmal's speech, I watched for their reaction. It was incredible. They never even blinked.

Finally, I closed my eyes and began to pray in English, to which they were accustomed. Then I prayed for several minutes in the language God had given me.

Muslims pray with their eyes open, so when I finished they were looking at me and smiling. Mr. Masoude spoke quietly, "That was beautiful."

On the way home that night, Julie squeezed my hand and said, "David, I still cannot believe how receptive they were to your praying in tongues."

I agreed. I was having trouble believing it myself.

Sometimes, on later occasions, God would lead me to pray in my prayer language with other Muslim friends. At times they would even request that I pray with them in my language from God.

Two years after that experience at the Masoudes' home, I learned that it is not unusual for a person in Islam who has a demonic problem to speak a language he has never learned. However, because I explained that this gift was from God, spoken in a normal way and taught in the Holy Bible, it was fully accepted.

Our time in Kabul was running out. We had been there two years, but still we didn't want to leave—especially now that I was finally beginning to communicate in Pushtu. More important than my language studies, however, were the meaningful relationships we had developed with several families. Our heavy-hearted good-byes to our Afghan friends were made even worse by the bleak possibility we would never again be able to return to their country.

The last night we were in Afghanistan in January 1979, I drove over to see Ajmal Masoude and his brothers. By this time they called me "the fourth brother."

I parked my old Volkswagen around the corner from their shop as a precaution and walked to their door.

Once inside the shop, we exchanged traditional greetings and I told them I desired to see them one last time before I left. For the first time in our friendship, conversation was awkward.

"I will pray for your health and safety," I mumbled.

"And we will pray for yours, Daoud," they responded.

We didn't talk much, for we knew that our conversation would bring about unacceptable tears. As a final farewell, we all stepped outside in front of the shop where I hugged each one, Afghan style, pausing for a second to look into their eyes. Their taut facial expressions told me their emotions, as mine, were in check only by the sheer strength of will.

Once in my car, I dropped my head on the steering wheel and let the tears fall.

The hardest part of love is the pain it sometimes brings—especially the pain of separation. I wept over the memory of this family and my memories of so many others. I wept about the happy times we had spent together, wondering if there would ever be such times again. I wept as I thought about their patience with my struggles in

Pushtu. The Masoude family had befriended me, taught me well, and loved me sincerely. They had received my gifts and given me theirs.

The words of Ajmal, spoken a few days earlier, once again came to mind. "Every night when Father comes from work he says to my youngest sister, 'Bring the Book to me.'" Thinking about those words brought tears once again.

After a while, I turned the key and the noisy, air-cooled engine whirred to life. Driving slowly home, I whispered a prayer patterned after Christ's own: "For I gave them the words you gave me" (John 17:8).

10

THE NIGHT THE NORTHERN ARMY CAME

We returned to the United States the end of January 1979. During the eight months we were there, we applied for residence visas to Pakistan because we knew of no way to obtain visas for Afghanistan. Though our hearts yearned to return to Afghanistan, the nation was now deeply embroiled in a war against the communist government. Resistance forces were springing up everywhere.

In September we received word from the Pakistani government that residence visas could not be granted to us. Firmly believing God would make a way for us where there seemed to be no way, we flew to Peshawar, Pakistan, with a 30-day tourist visa in our passports. We entered the country in mid-October, not knowing what we would do after the 30 days had expired.

To our complete amazement, during our first week in Peshawar we discovered a person could still apply for a tourist visa to Afghanistan. Few did because of the fighting and political instability. However, we went to the Afghan Consulate in Peshawar the next day and were granted 30-day tourist visas.

The seemingly impossible had happened. We stood with

our documents in hand, thrilled by the expectation of returning to Afghanistan. God had been good to us once again. Shortly after we received our visas, the Afghan government stopped issuing them.

A few days before we were to fly to Kabul, I had a terrible attack of paralyzing fear. It was understandable, I reasoned, to be apprehensive—even afraid. I knew Kabul was surrounded by *mujahideen*, the nationalist guerrillas, and that the situation would be very dangerous. But my fear was beyond anything rational; it was a horrifying, immobilizing terror.

In desperation, I said to Julie, "I'm not ready to go to Kabul yet. I'm too afraid. Let's shut ourselves in the hotel for three days and pray, fast, and read the Word. I've got to break this power of fear."

Although Julie was not experiencing the same fear as I, she was sympathetic and did not try to dissuade me.

For two days we fasted, prayed, and meditated on the Bible. On the second evening, as I was on my knees in earnest prayer, I began to see Afghanistan in my mind's eye as clearly as if I were there. I saw scenes I could not believe. The vision I had was so vivid and so real I could easily see every detail.

I saw patches of snow here and there, so I presumed it was spring but I was not sure. A river of troops in full battle dress poured from the north into Afghanistan. They came by the thousands, overwhelming the land. I saw fierce fighting in the streets of Kabul. Tanks were firing and distant smoke was rising throughout the city. I could almost smell the smoke and hear the sounds of the war. I saw myself walking down the street at dusk. I was going out of the city, looking over my shoulder to watch the angry, snarling tanks spitting fire from their cannons. Strangely, though my wife and I were seldom separated, Julie was not there. Yet I knew she was somewhere safe.

After a time, the scene before me became even more personal. In great detail I saw trees splintering, pieces of buildings spinning through the air and slamming into the dust, mothers searching for babies, and fathers trying vainly to protect the innocent. I heard screams of pain, children crying, and people gasping for air in the thick smoky haze. Blood flowed in the streets and panic swept through the neighborhoods, but there was no place to run or hide.

In my mind I was experiencing the anguish before it happened, and I fell on my face, agonizing and crying out to God for the city and the country I had come to love so much.

"God, show the Afghan people mercy," I pleaded. "Spare them from this agony and pain. I love them so, Lord. Must they suffer?"

As I was praying on the third night, I saw the exact same horrible drama played out in my mind's eye again. Then, a strange thing took place: My dominating fear was broken completely. It was replaced by a burden that caused me to care more for the people of Afghanistan than for David Leatherberry. It was as though God had pulled back the curtain and allowed me to see that in the most adverse circumstances He was able to keep us safe if He chose. It was not so much peace that overwhelmed me, but a distinct knowing I was to go there unafraid. My concern for the people made me forget my abnormal fear. Since God, not the fear, was in charge, I knew I would be there with my friends no matter what the consequences.

Upon our return to Kabul on November 6, 1979, I felt the warm emotions of coming home. The city had become my friend and to return to it was pleasant. At the airport we were greeted by Martin Gerald and his wife, Ruth, a wonderful couple who loved the Afghan people and had lived in Afghanistan for several years. They invited us to stay with them until we found housing.

I was full of excitement and anticipation to see Mr. Munsif, Ajmal Masoude, and other friends. Our return would be as surprising to them as our visas were to us.

Within a few days, Julie and I walked into the Masoude shop, acting but certainly not feeling casual. Rahman was sitting near the counter as usual. He was speechless when he saw us. Then his handsome face broke into a warm smile and he shouted out the back door to Ajmal and Khadim. When they came, we hugged and greeted each other joyously. Everybody was talking and asking questions at once. It was good to be with my brothers once again. Fortunately no one else was in the shop to inhibit our deeply personal homecoming.

"David, we didn't think you'd ever be able to come back to Afghanistan. We couldn't be happier to see you," Rahman said loudly. Then, lowering his voice, he warned, "David, things are even worse now. Kabul has changed. You must be careful. Watch who you talk to and where you go."

The others voiced their agreement with Rahman's words. Ajmal bit his lip, raised his eyebrows, and nodded as Khadim cast a furtive glance outside.

We left their shop, very happy to have seen them. Julie and I were eager to visit our other friends as well. However, to see the Masoude family in a public shop was quite simple; to visit a private home such as the Munsifs' would be a complicated matter. The Freedom Fighters were suspicious of any real or imaginary relationship with the communists, and the communists tended to arrest anyone they thought was connected with reactionaries or gangsters, their terms for the Freedom Fighters. The average citizen did not know whom to trust.

If we were to visit the Munsifs careful arrangements would have to be made. Through one of Mr. Munsif's cousins who worked in a hotel I sent a message that we had returned. Mr. Munsif sent a message warmly inviting us to visit him and his family the following Thursday evening. One of his relatives who owned a taxi would deliver us to his house. Our hearts were full of joy as we eagerly anticipated seeing our beloved teacher and friend.

When Thursday arrived, Julie and I dressed up for this very special occasion, according to Afghan tradition. I wore my fine *karakul* lambskin hat Mr. Munsif had given me one Christmas.

We left our house, walked four blocks to a main street, and flagged a taxi. The black-and-white Chevy stopped and we got in. At our request, the driver dropped us near some tourist shops. After browsing in the windows, we walked along Aziz's Street in the Shari Now area, watching for the Munsif cab. When it appeared, I flagged it down. Ten minutes later we arrived at a house owned by Mr. Munsif's father. The driver sounded the horn and the metal gates between the whitewashed walls quickly swung open. Once inside, the gates shut immediately and we faced a handsome, L-shaped, marble house that was mostly hidden from the view of anyone along the street.

We stepped out of the taxi into a beautiful garden as Mr. Munsif came out of the house. He embraced me and greeted Julie warmly. We hurried inside to a spacious room where his extended family members were ready to receive us. The warm glow of wall lights and a chandelier tempered the room's slight chill.

A festive meal had been prepared. It was served on a flowered cloth placed over an exquisite, handwoven Afghan carpet. Long sitting pads lined the sides of the cloth as Afghan tradition dictates. We feasted on *kabuli palau* (traditional rice topped with julienne carrots, raisins, and almonds with meat buried in the middle), lamb, chicken kabobs, Afghan meatballs, *burini* (fried eggplant cooked in a tomato sauce and topped with yogurt), and *nan* (bread). For dessert, we ate *firini*, a cooked, sweetened milk pudding spiced with cardamon and sprinkled with pistachios and ripe fruit. After the meal we sat together drinking hot black tea.

Reluctantly, after about three hours of stimulating conversation, we slipped away for an uneventful return home.

It was good to be back in Kabul.

After six weeks the possibility of our staying in Kabul seemed to improve, so we rented a nice three-room mud-brick house with a concrete floor. The small wood stove was enough to keep the winter cold out but not enough to really provide warmth or prevent the water pipes from freezing at times. We sometimes filled the house with more smoke than heat, but we had a phone and electricity so we were comfortable and needed nothing more.

My debilitating fear was gone. I wasn't going to run away. But because of God's preview, I felt especially sensitive to future events in Kabul. I had the same concerns any husband would have for his wife in such a situation, and the normal apprehensions at what I knew might occur still made me a bit edgy.

It was common knowledge, for example, the *mujahideen* could come into the city at any minute and shoot foreigners on sight thinking they were Russian advisors.

Will husky, bearded guerrillas leap over the wall that surrounds our house? I wondered.

In spite of God's assurance, some nights I lay awake very still, listening to every small sound. The quietness of the night seemed to hide dangers.

That's a brush of clothes against the wall, I would think. *Surely that's the creak of a sandal.* My heart would beat rapidly. The nights seemed as though they would never end.

On Christmas Eve 1979, while we were exchanging gifts with Martin and Ruth, Soviet troops and equipment began landing at the Kabul International Airport. At the time we didn't realize what was happening. We only knew for two nights it was difficult to sleep because of the constant drone of a large airplane circling overhead.

Throughout the day on both December 25 and 26 we saw what we thought was the same drab gray plane flying overhead. Later we learned we had witnessed the arrival of some of the 350 giant military transports coming from the Soviet Union. The Russian invasion of our beloved Afghanistan had begun.

About seven o'clock on the evening of December 27, Julie and I were finishing a holiday meal with two young Afghan guests. Though the holiday season was ours and not theirs, they had graciously accepted our invitation, and we were relaxing together and talking about God as we often did.

A distant explosion prompted us to run out of our

house to take a look. We had just raced out the door when a tremendous blast caused our whole area to shake.

How did the Freedom Fighters get those big weapons? I wondered.

"It sounds like serious trouble," I shouted to my friends. "You'd better get home as quickly as possible."

Julie and I prayed for their safety as they disappeared into the night.

I scrambled up to the flat roof of our house and crouched in the darkness. Trying to figure out what was happening, I stared through the barren branches of nearby trees as red tracer bullets filled the air. I listened as rockets shattered the normally quiet Afghan night. I strained to identify the various weapons in the deafening battle—the swish and boom of the rockets, the thunderous tank cannons, the rattle of automatic weapons, the crack of rifle fire.

Brilliant flares split the darkness high above me and I covered my eyes for protection. When my eyes readjusted to the darkness once again, I looked at the houses around ours. On nearly every housetop men were crouching in awe and fear of the deadly display.

At daybreak jet fighters crisscrossed the city flying at treetop level endeavoring to spread fear. Judging from my personal reaction, the fear tactics worked quite well. However, I felt compelled to take a short investigative walk.

As I proceeded down the street, I saw fair-haired, blue-eyed troops dressed in big fur hats and winter coats. They were carrying automatic weapons and guarding every street, crossroad, and mosque.

Russians, I thought. *It has happened. The invasion has occurred.*

Why hadn't that dawned on me? I asked myself as I hurried home.

We didn't think we would be able to remain in Afghanistan much longer, yet deep inside we hoped we could stay in the city that had been our home for almost three years. The few foreigners who had remained after the coup of '78 now rushed to get out of the country. Especially for an American, it was obviously no place to be.

About a week later I left our home to get groceries. The day was sunny and bright. Though it was cold, I didn't feel the chill as I walked the several blocks back to our house near the Rabbiah-Balkhi School. With my brown shoes, slacks, shirt, and blue ski jacket, I was identifiable as someone from the West. However, my dark blond hair, fair complexion, and blue eyes made me appear to be from the North—just like one of the hated Soviet soldiers.

I suddenly became aware of that similarity as I walked down the narrow street and met the icy stares of the rugged, mountain Afghans—people who only a week before had warmly greeted me in Pushtu or Dari. The dusty streets and mud-brick walls, with the neat houses hidden behind them, were the same, but the atmosphere was radically different.

The unusual quietness of the still-busy street made me feel alone. People talked in low voices. Though they glanced at me, no one would speak.

Before long I saw someone behind a wall look quickly at me then duck out of sight. As I realized what had happened, a cold fear crept into my mind. Was I being targeted by one of those famed Afghan marksmen? Having no desire to play hero or martyr, I stepped up my pace.

As I approached the curb to cross the street, a noisy bus rumbled slowly by. It was packed as usual. As it passed, all heads turned as one and every eye riveted on me with deep suspicion and disdain.

Given the chance, they'd kill me, I thought.

My mind turned to Julie. She was back at our mud-brick house alone. I knew because we were so close, so united in purpose, she would understand if something happened to me. Though her heart would be torn, she would not panic. She would carry on. We both knew the risks involved in our being here.

I walked to the lone, innocent chirp of a bird and wondered if I could hear the sound of a shot before I was struck. When a cat suddenly scampered up a tree, I jerked to protect myself.

Every cell in my body seemed to scream *run*. Yet I knew running would only increase the suspicion of those watching. Instead, I began to recall the linchpins of my life: My faith in God, built on the historical fact of Christ's resurrection, and my sure call from Him.

Though fear had reduced my life to a miniature, I realized I could not flee from this street, this city, or from Afghanistan. Being here was right, even though I had momentarily lost the feeling of God's presence. I walked on home knowing fear could not destroy the love I had for the Afghans, nor could it drive me away from their land.

Three weeks later, I waded out into the sparkling new snow blanketing the city. I walked down the street past the Russian soldiers. They stood out in their dark gray uniforms and fur hats with bright red stars in front. As I made my way along the near-empty sidewalk, some of them nodded as if they were greeting a fellow Russian.

I tried not to appear nervous, but my face felt hot and a rivulet of perspiration ran down my back. In my right hand I carried a basket with two New Testaments. I didn't want my two precious gifts confiscated.

Don't speak to me in Russian or I'll collapse, I thought as I walked by the soldiers.

When I finally passed the last sentry, I smiled politely. Within a couple of minutes I stepped into Saboor's workshop.

Saboor and I exchanged greetings. When we had finished, I said, "Saboor, may we step into your office for a second?"

"Of course," he said, ushering me inside. Though this tall, affable Afghan always wore greasy overalls, they did little to detract from his look of politeness and dignity.

"I know you are a devout man, so I have brought you an *Injil*, the Book that has changed my life," I said. "Unfortunately, it appears I will not be permitted to remain in Afghanistan much longer. This is the best present I know to give you."

After glancing outside of his office, I looked back at Saboor and said, "I believe you have the right to read it, although some may think differently."

As I spoke, I took out one of the New Testaments Julie had wrapped so carefully in a beautifully embroidered cloth.

Saboor politely took the gift and placed it on a high shelf behind him. He warmly shook my hand, and in a tone reflecting deep gratitude, he said, "Thank you so much."

I was warmed by his response and wanted to say more, but I knew I should not linger in his shop. I could only say, "You are welcome, Saboor. Good-bye, my friend."

He cleared his throat, looked at me and nodded. He understood.

I stepped into the street and headed for the tailor shop. While precariously picking my way up the snow-packed street, I thought about my friend Saboor. From the first time I stepped into his workshop he had been kind to me.

I will remember you as you read, Saboor, I silently promised.

I greeted the owner of the tailor shop as I entered. Although there were always people in his shop, on this day with such heavy snow the only person there was a day worker—a poor laborer with no steady employment who was just trying to keep warm.

I asked my friend behind the counter, "Would you mind asking this man to go buy some nice oranges for me?"

The broad-faced, heavy-set tailor spoke to the man. He gladly responded affirmatively so I gave the day laborer the necessary *afs* (coins).

When he left I said, "I will probably have to leave Afghanistan soon, and I have a special gift for you before I go. Because I know you believe in God, I want to give you an *Injil.*"

I handed it over the counter as I spoke. Still seated, he took it from me and put it underneath the counter. Then, with tears in his eyes, he jumped up from his chair, reached across the counter, and hugged me so hard I almost lost my breath.

"Thank you," he said.

"You are most welcome. I'm glad you are pleased," I replied.

When the day laborer returned, I took my oranges, said good-bye, and left. My emotions were heavy with gratitude. A sweet sadness spread through me as I walked toward my home.

Trudging past the Soviet soldiers in silence, not even caring if they spoke to me in Russian, I couldn't chase away the thought that perhaps I would never see my friends again. Once again my mind asked the question, *Lord, why can't I just live in Kabul, learn Pushtu fluently, and share Your love?*

11

UNEXPECTED COMPLIMENT

Julie and I had followed God's direction as faithfully as we knew how. The hard, irrevocable fact our visas were about to expire seemed inconsistent with His will. However, past experiences had proven we could trust God completely, so we once again prepared to leave Kabul.

During the first week in February 1980, Julie and I arrived at the Kabul Airport for our departure to Pakistan. We were alone. It was too dangerous for our Afghan friends to join us since the communists commonly considered Americans to be CIA agents. Security thoroughly checked both of us, as well as our luggage, before we were cleared to board the green-and-white, twin-prop Fokker that Pakistan International Airlines still flew between Kabul and Peshawar, Pakistan.

We buckled our seat belts and prepared for takeoff, my mind savoring the many wonderful memories of Mr. Munsif, Ajmal, and other Afghan friends. I silently prayed for each of them as our small aircraft taxied past tanks, trucks, huge troop transports, and the Soviet soldiers who stood guard out to the main runway.

Once airborne, we could clearly see the mammoth military camps set up in our beloved nation to house the Red Army. I desperately wished those black-looking camps standing in sharp relief to the new blanket of snow weren't there, but my wish did not change the scene below. My heart sank.

Am I really seeing this? I thought. I could hardly believe this had happened and we were in the middle of it.

Not wanting the sadness to overwhelm me, I forced myself to consider Pakistan and the opportunities God might have waiting for us there. Our 50-minute trip soon ended. With one bounce of the aircraft we were on the airstrip in Peshawar, not far from the mouth of the famous Khyber Pass.

Our bags cleared customs and I found a taxi to take us to Jan's (pronounced John's) Hotel. I knew better than to allow the taxi driver to set the price or to hassle with him at the end of the trip. When that happened, either the cabbie tended to get nasty or the trip very expensive. Therefore, we agreed on a price beforehand and had an uneventful, quiet ride to our hotel on Islamia Road.

Jan's was an older, three-story hotel long past its prime. However, it was moderately priced and functional. We chose a corner room on the top floor because it was a little larger than the others and gave us easy access to the roof. Julie could hang our wash on a line stretched between two water heaters. Those water heaters were another important reason for our selecting Jan's—we knew we could count on a hot shower.

The medium-sized room had two small windows. One was covered by an orange curtain; the other contained an air conditioning unit that produced an incredible amount of sound and a very small amount of cool air. The walls were painted off-white; a well-worn carpet, originally a green floral, covered the floor. Electric wires ran under the carpet and up the wall to various outlets and to the lone lamp in the corner. Surprisingly, the electrical system was strong enough to allow us to make tea in our hot pot without blowing a fuse. The two single beds were made up with clean sheets, hard pillows, and army-type blankets. As we took it all in, we saw very quickly everything in the room was well used.

The rooms were arranged in a rectangle, each facing an atrium with a skylight at the center of the roof. This configuration made an alarm clock unnecessary, for at five o'clock every morning tea was served in the atrium. The sounds of talking waiters pushing rattling carts on the marble floors rose like smoke up a chimney, filtering into every room and awakening everyone.

The restaurant on the ground floor served a free breakfast to the guests. The food was good and the kind, friendly treatment by the hotel staff made our stay at Jan's enjoyable, in spite of the other deficiencies.

Across the street from the hotel, drivers with *tongas* (two-wheeled, horse-drawn buggies) stood ready to whisk shoppers anywhere in the city. Once bargaining over the price of the ride was complete, the driver would give a sharp command to the horse and away they would go. Both the driver and the rider normally think they have gotten the best price, but actually the driver usually comes out on top.

Also on the street were rickshaw-type, three-wheeled public scooters. These machines were motorized and had low, overhead roll bars. Julie and I nicknamed them "MIGs on wheels." The wild rides we experienced in those vehicles often caused me to bump my head. That would prompt me to tap the driver on the shoulder and remind him, "I only have one life to live. Please be careful."

We didn't know it when we first arrived, but Jan's Hotel was to be our off-and-on home for the next 13 months. Because we couldn't get permanent visas for Pakistan during those 13 months, we had to make several trips to India using tourist visas from Pakistan and India to stay near the Pushtun people we loved.

Most days in Peshawar were sunny and bright, and the day Julie and I chose to ride with our friend Roger White to the Afghanistan border was no exception.

Roger pulled up in front of Jan's in his rough and ready Land Rover. His 6'2" frame sprang out of the vehicle almost before it stopped. As we shook hands, my hand nearly disappeared in Roger's. This broad-shouldered Englishman was a big man in every way—including his heart. His quick smile accented the freckles and crinkle lines around his eyes, both of which contributed to a very friendly demeanor.

"Hello," he greeted us warmly.

After exchanging some pleasantries, the three of us loaded into his Land Rover and took off. We left Peshawar and wound our way through the 25-mile Khyber Pass toward the Pakistani checkpoint at Torkham.

The bouncing, four-wheel-drive vehicle brought to mind earlier trips Julie and I had made between Kabul and Peshawar. Those trips, however, were made on the silver bullet bus—so named because the silver-gray vehicle made the trip at breakneck speeds through some beautiful, yet treacherous mountain terrain.

I remembered the border crossing as a bustling, friendly spot where conversation was easily exchanged between both officials and travelers. Yet when we arrived that day, we encountered radical changes. Armed Pakistani border guards and Afghan soldiers stood facing each other with only a short stretch of barbed wire separating them.

Momentarily defying that sharp restraint, I reached across the barbed wire and shook hands with the Afghan soldiers as I greeted them in Pushtu. They smiled and warmly returned my greetings, apparently happy someone had reached out to them. Their warmth reminded me they were simply Afghans caught in a cultural and political dilemma.

Julie and I left the border and trekked up a small hill where we could see farther into Afghanistan. Even from that elevation, the oasis-like view had been changed by the war. I thought I could see the burned spot where a helicopter was rumored to have been shot down during earlier fighting. Looking toward the guardhouse and customs building among a group of trees on the Afghan side, I let my eyes travel the road between the two customs checkpoints. Among the trees on the Pakistani side, I could see several buildings that housed restroom facilities and places to buy gifts or refreshments. Only a trickle of people passed through the Afghan checkpoint 200 yards away.

For old times' sake, I strained to see if I could locate anything familiar. Then I thought about our friends in Afghanistan. They were so close—maybe only 155 miles away—yet so far.

I want to go back, yet I can't because of the political barrier brought about by the war, I thought sadly.

From our bench seat on the hill, we looked longingly at the land we loved so very much. Julie wondered out loud about Mrs. Munsif and her daughters, as well as other friends in Kabul who had been so kind. They could do nothing to prevent what was occurring in their country. They could only wait inside their homes while the soldiers wasted the land outside.

Unable to prevent tears from flowing as we continued to stare at our beloved land, I walked to a small tree nearby. Again I looked toward barren, beautiful Afghanistan. I prayed with all of my heart the Lord Jesus Christ would help our friends who were suffering there.

Questions began to fill my mind—questions that plague the human race.

Why do babies have to die? Why are defenseless men,

women, and children shot? Homes are destroyed and land is laid waste. Why? What about those who take advantage of their fellow countrymen when they are vulnerable, those who deceive and betray their own? How can they do this and still live with themselves?

I breathed deeply, looked toward the blue sky where a few white clouds drifted near the mountains, and continued my questioning.

What makes men lie, steal, kill, and wound? Where do lust and thirst for power come from? Is selfishness in every man's heart?

I knew it was. God calls such rebellion against Him sin, and every person is guilty. I knew the universal problem of sin would not go away. Mankind's treatment of each other will always result in betrayal and pain unless we repent, ask for God's forgiveness, and accept His life-changing love.

"God," I said softly, "I know You care because You came to earth in the flesh to suffer ultimate torture and pain for every person's sin. Please enable me to help others understand this truth."

Turning away from my beloved Afghanistan, I walked back toward Julie. Dabbing away her tears, she rose from the bench as I approached. Unable to speak, I just looked into her soft brown eyes. Understanding the thoughts I could not verbalize, she briefly touched her hand to mine. Our trip down the stony path to meet Roger was quiet and reflective.

While Julie and I were up on the hill, Roger had walked around and talked to border officials. Seeing we had returned, he greeted us cheerfully. Quickly he sensed our sadness and motioned for us to get in the Land Rover. We drove home in silence.

As our temporary visas for Pakistan were about to expire

again, we prepared for yet another trip to India.

Ghalmaghal (Pushtu for noise and confusion) was the order of the day when we arrived at the Lahore airport. We checked in our bags, cleared passport control, went through the security checks, and entered the huge preboarding room to wait for our flight. Once in the room we saw between 15 and 20 rugged-looking Pushtuns waiting to also board the plane for India. Both by their appearance and their actions it was obvious these bearded men had not often traveled by plane. In fact, they probably had never flown before.

I walked over and greeted one of them, a powerfully built man with a full red beard. His eyes registered surprise when I spoke to him in his mother tongue. His response in soft Pushtu made me think he was from Kandahar, a large Pushtun city in southeast Afghanistan. Our conversation was cut short by the boarding call in Urdu (the national language of Pakistan) and English.

As the Indian Airlines Boeing 737 lifted off the runway, the cabin attendants were frantically trying to seat the Pushtun group. However, these men continued to walk the aisles, peering out the windows and talking loudly to one another. One huge, black-bearded Pushtun finally stepped over the back of a seat to the next row and sat down.

When the seat belt sign went off, I unbuckled mine and walked back to where two of the Pushtuns were seated and asked if I could sit down.

They replied that I could, then asked if I would help them fill out the necessary disembarkation forms. The one in the group seated next to me watched me in silence. To his right was the red-bearded man I had first met.

Desiring to start a conversation about God, I inquired of them both, "Do you gentlemen believe in Almighty God?"

"Do we believe in God?" they repeated in unison as

though it were an incredulous question. They proceeded to tell me how strongly they believed, forcefully slapping their right hands over their hearts in the strong, enthusiastic Pushtun manner.

"That's wonderful," I said. "I do too."

They seemed genuinely surprised that I believed as firmly in God as they.

"Have you ever seen or read the *Injil*?" I inquired. When they shook their heads no, I said, "Would you be interested in looking at one?"

"Oh yes, definitely," they assured me in the same emphatic manner. So I reached into my briefcase and gave them a copy of the big, bulky Pushtu New Testament.

They looked at the book for a moment and touched it lightly, but it was soon obvious that they couldn't read. We were all embarrassed, but before I knew what to say they passed the New Testament back one row to a young university student who began to read.

After a few moments the student exclaimed to those around him, "I have just been given a beautiful gift!"

I said, "It's wonderful you can read God's Holy Book. You will want to read this to all of the men, wherever you go. Please read this to them, will you?"

"Yes," he replied. "I most certainly will."

When we deplaned in New Delhi, I saw the student carry the New Testament off the plane in a plastic airline tote bag. He was carefully holding the large book above his waist because in his culture it would be disrespectful to carry a holy book below the belt line.

He waited for me outside customs until my bags cleared. Approaching me, he very politely said, "I really want to thank you for this, and I want to give you a gift to show my appreciation."

He handed me the small bag of peanuts he had received
from the airline because that was the only thing he had
to give. He then shook my hand and disappeared into the
crowd.

How could you not love people like this? I pondered.

Julie and I made several trips to India over the next few
months, but I knew we could not keep up this hopeless visa
circle indefinitely. It wasn't so much the weariness and incon-
venience of constantly traveling back and forth that brought
discouragement to us; it was the fact we didn't have enough
time to build lasting relationships.

When I didn't know what to do next, God touched my life
in a way I would never have expected.

Once again we had returned to Jan's Hotel from India, and
I was discouraged. One Sunday morning I went downstairs,
left the hotel, and walked the few blocks to Khalid Park.
I was weary and frustrated about our seemingly hopeless
situation. To make matters worse, that morning Julie and I
had a rare, but serious, misunderstanding. I say it was rare
because in all of our 17 years of marriage we had seldom
had strong disagreements.

Khalid Park is a pleasant place to relax and enjoy the col-
orful flowers that border the well-kept grassy areas. I took a
seat on one of the concrete benches across the street from a
small mosque. Birds sang their melodies from the mammoth
trees scattered throughout the park, but their happy-sound-
ing chirps mocked my solemn mood.

In my frustration, I decided the only fair thing to do was to
hand in my resignation to the Lord.

"Lord," I began, "I just don't have what it takes. You
made a big mistake calling me to work for You. Lord, I just
want to live among the Pushtuns, to whom You have called

me and given me such a great love, but I can't. I'm unable to get a permanent visa right now, and to live there wouldn't do much good anyway because I'm not fluent in the Pushtu language—even after hundreds of hours of study. Lord, I'm simply not effective for You in Asia. I'm less than average and certainly not worthy of all the people who make it possible for me to be here. And, Lord, I don't have the slightest idea what to do next."

Trying to honestly face the issue, I continued: "Lord, I don't want to be an embarrassment to You or others. Besides all that, Lord, I've discouraged and hurt the person I love the most—Julie. I'm sorry, Lord, but I just don't have what it takes. So this morning I'd like to hand in my resignation."

I fully expected the Lord to nod and say, "Well, yes, David, you're right." Instead, I heard very different words—quiet yet most definitely clear and intensely personal.

David, I am the Person who chooses and calls. I don't make mistakes. I'm not accepting your resignation. You have been faithful in answering My call and being obedient to Me. I want you to know this morning, I deeply appreciate that.

That God was speaking to me did not surprise me nearly as much as what He said. I thought He would most certainly agree with me. Instead, He complimented me! Such a compliment was completely unexpected.

The quiet communion continued: *Don't worry, David. I am going to work all of these things out for your good and My glory. You don't understand all of this now, but you will later. You are in the center of My will.*

All worldly sounds, from the chirp of the birds to the roar of the nearby traffic, were blocked from my ears and mind. I was aware of nothing but God's presence. Amazed and awed by His powerful presence, love, and grace, I sat there surrounded with a feeling of total acceptance.

My heart was flooded with joy. Christ would not accept my resignation! He still wanted me! I sat for a few minutes longer, basking in the warm feeling God's words had brought, savoring the glow of the present.

Loving parents compliment as well as correct their child, and they do not wait until the child is perfect to do so, I thought. There was something special about God saying good things to me about me.

I rose from the bench, eager to share this good news with Julie.

Entering our room, I took her hands, looked into her eyes, and said simply, "Forgive me, Julie."

With a forgiving smile she replied, "Oh, David."

"Honey," I continued, "I tried to hand in my resignation and the Lord wouldn't accept it."

"I understand," she answered. "I felt like doing the same."

Excitedly I added, "But, Honey, we're going to make it!"

"I know, David," she said softly. "I know."

In detail, I told Julie what had happened. I explained how God's compliment had lifted and encouraged me. I knew we were in His will and could depend on His leading.

We bowed our heads in prayer.

"I thank You, Lord, for an understanding wife," I began. "Forgive me for hurting her. I never want to do it again. Thank You that we have each other. Thank You also for letting me know I am of value to You and Your kingdom work. Amen."

12

PESHAWAR ENCOUNTERS

Encouraged by God himself, Julie and I felt refreshed and strengthened. Still, we had no residence visas and no apartment. In fact, we didn't know how long we could remain in Pakistan. Yet even though we couldn't get a permanent visa, we had a keen sense we were meeting the people God desired. To please God and to be in the center of His will gave us deep satisfaction, making it possible for us to relax and enjoy living at Jan's Hotel as long as was necessary.

Versatile Julie had learned to live out of a suitcase and to make any place home. At Jan's she washed clothes in the sink, hung them on the rooftop, and ironed them on the desk with a travel iron. She made tea in our electric hot pot, and was resourceful and inventive as our other needs arose. I was grateful to have a wife whose happiness did not depend on possessions.

As the days came and went, I spent time walking through the bazaars of Peshawar, meeting Pushtuns and other residents and observing their ways so I might relate to them by developing a better understanding of their culture.

Late one afternoon, I met a pleasant-looking Pakistani medical intern named Ahmad. After talking with me briefly, he invited me to his house for tea. The ride to his home on the back of his motorcycle was the beginning of a lasting friendship.

As we sipped our tea, Ahmad talked about his family and studies as well as his hospital intern experiences. Never having been inside Peshawar's well-known Lady Reading Hospital, I was glad when Ahmad asked if I wanted to tour it.

"I truly want to help my people," he told me later as we walked down the hospital hallway. He seemed completely sincere, and I could sense he was not in medicine for money or prestige. He simply wanted to help his people, to lift them up.

A few weeks later Ahmad called from the hospital with an urgent message that a nomadic Afghan refugee named Bibigul had just given birth to a daughter and needed a blood transfusion. Earlier I had told Ahmad that Julie and I were willing to give blood if needed. Since Julie had the right blood type for Bibigul, she headed for the hospital immediately.

As Julie rode in the rickshaw, anxious about the situation she would find at the hospital, she prayed for the mother and baby she had never seen. "God, I know You love Bibigul and this new little life. Help everything medically to work out right and may this blood I give be a gift of life from You," she prayed earnestly.

The rickshaw jolted about that time and raised her off the seat. She almost struck her head on the roll bar. *Glad I'm shorter than David,* she thought.

Then, returning to her prayer, she said, "Lord, there are so many Pushtu dialects. Please help me to understand this woman who may be more frightened than I am. Let me talk with ease, Lord, and remember the right words."

With a final bump, the rough-riding vehicle stopped. She paid the driver and entered the hospital.

An hour later, Julie bolted through our door and fairly skipped across the room. Ecstatically she proclaimed, "David, mother and new baby are fine! And Bibigul and I can understand each other beautifully!"

On a subsequent visit, a thankful Bibigul asked Julie if she had any children of her own.

Julie smiled and replied, "No. My husband and I love children, but God has not yet chosen to give us a child. *Khoodai da rawki* (May God give us children)."

She then told Bibigul she had been a first-grade teacher for seven years. These words of explanation ended the conversation, but Julie knew Bibigul felt deep sadness for her. In the Afghan culture, for a wife not to have a son is a grave concern to her because the son becomes the provider for his elderly parents. To be childless is often considered a curse.

Before she left Bibigul, Julie heard the same familiar words that had been spoken to her so often by other Muslim women. "I will pray that you will have a child," Bibigul said.

Tenderly looking into Bibigul's eyes, Julie's response let her know she accepted her concern. "Thank you, Bibigul," Julie said. "You are kind."

A variety of people continued to cross our path at Jan's Hotel. Kareem was a delightful fellow, about 19 years old. Every time I saw Kareem he had a wide grin on his face. Tall, sinewy, and usually dressed in a suit-vest over his more typical Afghan shirt and trousers, he moved with quickness.

Kareem always appeared happy. Never once did he fail

to greet me with the question "Daoud, you happy? You happy?" His happy demeanor prompted us to refer to him as "Mr. Happy." He visited me often, wanting to practice English. He would also bring papers he had written for me to correct. His cheerful way brightened my day.

Early one afternoon on the rooftop of Jan's, while precariously sitting on a couple of dilapidated, wooden-framed chairs, I asked Kareem a question.

"Do you know ... are you absolutely sure when you die you will go to heaven?" I inquired. Though we had talked about God many times, I had never asked my young friend such a question.

"Oh, Daoud, nobody can know that," Kareem replied. "Only God knows that. Only God knows where you are going."

"But Kareem, I know for sure when I die I am going to heaven," I responded.

"Oh, don't say that, Mr. Daoud. You don't know." He shook his head so vigorously he nearly lost his rolled-up Nuristani cap. Then he repeated, "You cannot know that. Only God knows that." Then he continued, "You are arrogant, very arrogant and presumptuous to say that."

"Kareem, you're right. I would be very arrogant and presumptuous if I said myself that I am going to heaven, but when God says to me in His Holy Bible that I can know for sure, who am I to question God?"

He looked very thoughtful for a moment, then slowly shook his head as if he were struggling with his thoughts. The dilemma of believing what was inside him and believing words from the Holy Bible clashed in his mind. However, those struggles never kept him away from me. As long as we stayed at Jan's, Kareem continued to visit me for English lessons and long talks about God.

Another person I encountered during our stay in Peshawar was Abdul Mohammed Khan, a retired Pakistani military officer who had fought in Burma during World War II. The opposite of Kareem, he was a gruff, constant complainer who usually offended people because he was so uninterested in them. When I was first introduced to Mr. Khan, he acted as though I was simply an interruption in his day. I did not give him much thought after that meeting because he obviously was not interested in getting acquainted.

During that summer, Julie and I house sat for a friend who rented from Mr. Khan, and this gruff Pakistani would occasionally come to the house to check up on things. One time I ran into him unexpectedly as I came around the corner of the building. To my surprise, the instant I saw him I felt this directive from the Spirit of God: *Make Mr. Khan your friend.* So I attempted to do just that.

After a while I came to like him despite his brash, sometimes insulting way and military manner. I had concluded his manner was just a defensive front. He was a wealthy man who, except for servants, lived alone in a house that was not overly ostentatious but certainly reflected his means.

Eventually he invited me to his home for the first of what would turn out to be several visits and sometimes elegant dinners. There, amid expensive objects of art and oriental carpets, I listened to his opinions about the British (whom he despised), and the Americans and Russians (who, according to him, strove for world supremacy and were responsible for most of the world's ills). He derided almost everything, except God.

I discovered he was an avid reader. His library shelves

were packed with books on a wide range of subjects—
from military history in Asia to the writings of Shakespeare, whom he often quoted. This fascinated me since I
knew how much he disliked the British. However, he did
not seem to be aware of the inconsistency between his
words and his actions.

One time, while visiting with Mr. Khan, he unexpectedly said to me, "Why do you care about me the way you
do? Why do you bother with me?"

I first wondered how to respond, then I felt the Lord
wanted me to tell him about the day the Spirit of God
said, *Make him your friend.*

I thought Mr. Khan might not believe me or perhaps
even ridicule me, but to my surprise he said, "Really, is
that what God said to you?"

"Yes," I said.

On two other occasions he said to me, "David, please
tell me again about the day God told you to make me
your friend."

Each time I recalled the same details.

That day is important to him, I thought. *Why?*

I absolutely never knew what to expect from Mr. Khan
when I met with him.

"I want to read the whole Bible," he said one day. "Can
you get me a copy?"

"Sure."

He later told me he was spending the greater part of
each afternoon reading the Bible. From time to time,
he would tell me what he had read. The biblical tribal
customs were especially interesting to him. He mentioned
how Abraham made his servant promise to select a bride
for his son Isaac from his own tribe by the custom of
placing his hand under Abraham's thigh. Mr. Khan said

he knew of a Pushtun tribe that practices similar oath-binding today.

On one afternoon visit, as soon as I was ushered into the house by his servant, Mr. Khan raised his voice and shouted angrily, "You followers of Christ are yellow-bellied cowards! No backbone!"

As usual I was caught off guard.

"What's wrong, Mr. Khan?" I asked.

In a controlled rage, his dark eyes shot accusations. Still shouting at me he said, "Do you know what I read in the New Testament today? Those lousy disciples of Jesus deserted Him in the Garden of Gethsemane! I really like Jesus, but His followers are no-good deserters! We Pushtuns would have stood and fought!"

I was at a loss for words, not because I had no answer but because his fury took my breath away. I tried to explain Jesus did not allow them to fight in the Garden, and that after the Resurrection and the Day of Pentecost a great change took place in His disciples.

"The Book of Acts in the Bible shows the disciples' tremendous boldness and courage," I told him, adding he would discover this if he would keep reading. However, I don't think his anger allowed him to hear a single word I said that day.

Sometime later Mr. Khan invited me over for an evening meal. He said he had finished reading the Bible. Never had I seen him so calm and thoughtful as he was that evening. Slowly he ran his hand through his thinning, graying hair, then leaned toward me and said ever so softly, "What I read in the New Testament sounds so good. In fact, it sounds too good—it just cannot be true."

For the first time, I caught a glimpse of a different Mr. Khan. He was simply a lonely man who wanted to find hope, something he had lost at some time in his life. His past accomplishments meant little to him. His life had become empty and meaningless.

I leaned forward and said, "I know it sounds too good to be true, but it is true. That's the beauty of it."

For a long time he sat motionless and silent, looking intently on my face in the perceptive Pushtun way, watching for any sign of doubt or betrayal.

Finally he whispered, "I wish it were true."

"It is," I said.

Three months after we left Pakistan, Mr. Khan died.

Often I walked the short distance from Jan's to Khalid Park, my "study," where I read books or worked on Pushtu. One day, while sitting on my favorite bench, I looked a short distance across the park and saw three men standing with their backs to me. They appeared to be Afghan *mujahideen.*

I was about to return to my book when out of the blue these words were strongly impressed on my mind: *David, in a little while those three men are going to turn around and walk over to you. I want you to explain to them My way to the path of life.*

I thought, *Lord, I don't believe that's wise. I don't know them.* As there was no response to my thought, I simply dropped my head and tried to concentrate on my work once again.

A short time later, as I glanced over the top of my book, I saw three sets of sandaled feet with toes pointed toward me. Taken aback, I raised my eyes to see those three Afghan men, dressed in the traditional fare—loose-fitting pants and shirts and a vest, topped off with black turbans—standing before me. The one in the middle was a huge, muscular man. The one on the right was just as tall but wiry. The other was of medium build and height. They all had mustaches, and, thankfully, they had what Afghans call open faces (pleasant looks).

I gained my composure.

"*Asalaam alekum* (Peace be upon you)," I said.

"*Wali kum salaam* (And peace be upon you also)," they responded.

The tall man, Mahmood, spoke in broken English. He told me they once attended Kabul University but were now *mujahideen*. As tough as they were, their attitude toward me could not have been kinder. In the most natural way, we almost immediately started talking about Almighty God. They were surprised to find I believed in God, for they thought—as many do—that Westerners don't genuinely believe in God. One asked me if we could meet again.

"I would like that," I said.

Mahmood asked, "Can you teach us English?"

"Sure."

As it was not workable for them to meet with me at the hotel, we decided to meet in the park.

In our hotel room, I wrote an English lesson and Julie typed it. I then had copies made of the lesson and taught it to the men. Every day we repeated the process, and three to five additional men who had been invited by the original three joined us. The arrangement seemed good for my Pushtu and their English, but I can only imagine how it appeared to onlookers as six or eight rugged-looking men sat in a semicircle in front of me. I would say in a loud voice, "Please repeat after me: The boy ran up the hill."

This was enthusiastically followed by a manly chorus,

"The boy ran up the hill."

Then I would say, "The boy ran down the hill."

"The boy ran down the hill," repeated the men in unison.

We had a great time turning Khalid Park into a classroom.

Sometimes, right in the middle of a lesson, it would be time for their prayers. They left the semicircle, lined up facing Mecca, put their faces to the ground, and prayed. I respectfully waited until they finished, then we would continue our lesson.

About four weeks later, the temporary Pakistani visas Julie and I had were about to expire. During our next-to-the-last time together, I asked the men if they had seen or were interested in the Holy Bible, the *Injil*. "I'll give you a copy if you would like to have one," I told them.

Four of them requested one.

I had to bid my new friends good-bye, knowing they would soon return to battle, and perhaps death, in Afghanistan. It was a difficult farewell. I hugged each *mujahid* and reassured him by saying, "You will be in my prayers."

13

DEAD BOLT DOORS

That we were not going to be granted permanent visas for Pakistan was at first perplexing to me and very upsetting to Julie. Together we carefully looked at our options.

We had heard West Germany was receiving Afghan refugees and that the population had reached 20,000-25,000 in Frankfurt alone. After we spent time in prayer and consideration, West Germany seemed like a logical place for us to go.

Though I felt comfortable with the decision, Julie did not. She just couldn't believe we were leaving Asia. I tried to comfort Julie by assuring her we could eventually return to Pakistan. Though our hearts were in Afghanistan, being able to return to Kabul still looked impossible.

"We just have to take another step of faith and believe God will be with us," I said one evening when Julie seemed especially discouraged.

Although we had never been to Germany and had no idea what we would do there, whom to contact, or where to live, we knew Afghans were there and we were confident God would help us.

Our sponsoring church, the Assemblies of God, approved our relocation plans. Once again I was grateful for this kind of cooperation that allowed us to move with some autonomy.

Armed with my sense that this was right for us, we boarded a plane in Peshawar to fly to Karachi and then on to

Frankfurt. As the plane lifted off from the runway, I looked at Julie's sad countenance, squeezed her hand, and said, "We'll be back, Sweetie. We'll be back."

"Uh huh," she said without conviction. Leaning back against the seat with her eyes closed, she let the tears flow down her cheeks.

We arrived in Frankfurt in March 1981.

After clearing passport control and picking up our bags, Julie peered at a map of the city, pondering where we should go. Meanwhile I dialed the relative of a German friend who had been in Afghanistan. The German/English conversation netted me one fact: my friend was in the United States.

Bone tired and frustrated, we finally got a cab to downtown Frankfurt in search of a hotel room. Unprepared for the high prices of Western Europe, we thought at first we were being taken advantage of as tourists. After lugging our suitcases to several hotels and finding the price unchanged, we paid for a room and went to bed.

The next day I called John Koeshall, an acquaintance from the United States who worked in Munich with German college students. His wife, Anita, informed me he was at a conference but gave me the phone number of another American couple, Cary and Faye Tidwell. She said they might be able to help us.

That evening the Tidwells had dinner with us. With only a few hours to spend together, they did their best to orient us to the German culture and the city of Frankfurt.

The following day we began looking for an Afghan named Jamil. His address had been given to me by a mutual friend in Pakistan. Julie and I found him living in a hotel about 15 minutes from us. We introduced ourselves, mentioning our friend in Pakistan. Jamil warmly received us, apologizing that his wife and baby weren't home.

During our visit, we were impressed by Jamil's warmth, intelligence, and concern for his people. I could see why this man had been such a respected professor at Kabul University. Eventually I felt comfortable enough with Jamil to ask his counsel.

"Would it be a good idea if Julie and I offered to teach English to Afghans who plan to go to the United States?" I inquired.

He thought teaching was the most practical thing we could do, and he asked several questions about us and our abilities. Because of the recommendation I had from my friend in Pakistan, and because Jamil had known other Americans who truly loved God, he immediately accepted us as people who wanted to help Afghans. We left his room encouraged and with great anticipation in our hearts.

On our third day in Germany we received a phone call from an American named Diane McCarty. While talking with Faye Tidwell about us, Diane had asked, "Do they need a place to stay? As you know, Roy, the girls, and I enjoy helping like that."

"Well, yes, they do need a place to stay," Faye had responded.

"Then have them come and stay in our house if they will," Diane said.

What lengths God goes to provide for us, I thought when I heard the news.

Happily Julie and I agreed to stay with the McCarty family.

When we arrived at their home the next day, Diane said we would be in their teenage daughter's downstairs room. Our immediate response was to decline such sacrifice. However, their daughter Karen's giving attitude prompted us to accept the McCartys' gracious hospitality.

"No problem," said the teen with an impish grin. "Mom and I already talked about it. I just l-o-o-o-v-e to sleep in the living room!"

The people of Frankfurt—like Germans as a whole—are clean, orderly, private people. To those who are unfamiliar with their culture, they can appear quite distant. To protect the privacy and quiet of their homes and apartments, the doors are very heavy. When locked with a dead bolt, those doors seem impenetrable. Julie and I felt our situation was not unlike those locked doors.

Other Americans heard about us and were concerned. They knew how difficult it was to find housing in Frankfurt. We soon learned other foreigners had searched for months without success.

Were we just naive? Had we made a mistake? Were we looking at unyielding, dead bolt doors? These questions ran through my mind more than once.

One of the rental agencies we called told us that multitudes were looking for places to live in Frankfurt. Before hanging up they said, "Call back next month."

Another told us, "We don't have anything to show you."

The answers from almost all of the agencies were basically the same. What was even worse, rental agencies were charging renters a fee of two- to three-months' rent, plus a security deposit—also equal to two- to three-months' rent—that went to the owner. In addition, the contract usually stipulated a one- or two-year minimum rental period; and when the apartment was vacated, it had to be in newly decorated condition or the renter had to pay for total redecoration.

To say we couldn't afford all that was an understatement.

"I think we can find a place by just walking around and looking," I declared to Jamil and his family one day.

Kindly offering to go with Julie and me, Jamil replied, "Let's walk around this neighborhood."

Within minutes, we were dwarfed by two glass-and-steel apartment buildings. These buildings were 16 and 13 stories high with interconnecting hallways. We entered the smaller one. Jamil, who knew enough German to get by, asked the *hausmeister* (apartment manager) if anything was available to rent.

"Yes," a man said. "But you have to go downtown to the managing office."

As quickly as possible, Julie and I took a bus to the downtown office. We were confronted by a tall, slender, no-nonsense secretary.

"We're looking for an apartment," I told her through the translator who had been brought in to deal with us.

"I'll make arrangements for you to look at one," the secretary replied in German, picking up the phone.

As she dialed, I informed the translator (who in turn told the secretary), "We may want the apartment for only six months. I don't want to sign a longer contract because I don't know for sure how long we'll be here. We must be ready to return to Pakistan."

The secretary angrily put the phone down. With a why-are-you-wasting-my-time attitude, she coldly replied, "Well, there's no use looking at it. We can't do anything for you."

I silently prayed as we walked to the door and started to leave. Quite suddenly and unexpectedly the secretary said, "Wait a minute." She paused, cocking her head to the right. Then, looking thoughtfully into space, she continued, "The owner of the apartment complex should be back in three days. Come in and maybe you can talk with him."

We stood there puzzled until the translator relayed the message. We thanked her and left the building, moderately encouraged by her last statement.

For the next three days, I prayed at every opportunity for this apartment landlord I had never met. I prayed more for the man than for our need for an apartment.

On the scheduled day, we returned to the downtown office complex with our own translator, a lovely, Christian woman. When we arrived, the curt secretary ushered us inside the man's large, private office. I was surprised to see his office had such plain appointments. Black furniture and a cloudy day gave a dark appearance to the otherwise functional interior.

Mr. John Wanewski, a man in his early fifties, came around his big wooden desk to shake hands and offer us chairs. His dark blue business suit heightened the blueness of his eyes. His dark hair, graying at the temples, added to his distinguished looks. He appeared to be a warm person who was not preoccupied by his own wealth.

Our German translator told him we had been working in Afghanistan and he seemed quite interested, nodding his head occasionally. His questions about my motivation for assisting Afghans led into a conversation about God. I learned his father had been a devout rabbi in Poland. Mr. Wanewski himself had come to West Germany as a refugee with the equivalent of a dollar in his pocket. Later an associate in the office told us Mr. Wanewski now owned 17 buildings in Frankfurt. He also mentioned Mr. Wanewski had offices in New York City.

Our discussion, which lasted about an hour, turned to wealth and its meaning. He related its importance was less than people thought because, "When a person dies, he cannot take one dollar with him." Then a smile crossed his face. His eyes, while not hard, were not happy either as he stated, "Wealth has no lasting value."

Mr. Wanewski politely brought our conversation to a close, and then asked, "Now what is your need regarding an apartment?"

"I'd like to have an apartment that is undecorated on a six-month lease. I would also like the option of staying beyond that length of time for as long as I need with only a 30-day notice required before I leave," I stated matter-of-factly, talking as if I had not just asked for the most unreasonable contract in all of Frankfurt. "Also, I would like to have my security deposit returned on the day I leave."

My spirit soared when he replied, "Fine, come out here to my secretary and I'll dictate the terms to her. Anything you want in the contract, I'll write it in."

He never so much as blinked during the entire procedure. However, his secretary flinched at nearly every line of the contract she typed.

As we left the building and walked out into the street, our joy bubbled over—not so much because of the apartment, but because of Mr. Wanewski's openness. My mind continued to ponder as I thought about this kind man who seemed so sincerely hungry for God.

Our translator was overwhelmed by what she had just seen. "It's unheard of," she said.

Though I knew she was probably right in most situations, I thought to myself, *How easily the Lord opens doors that outwardly appear to be impenetrable because of dead bolt locks!*

I needed to see an immigration official about obtaining a residence visa for Germany, so within a few days after arriving in Frankfurt I made my way to a government office building on Mainzer Landstrasse. Finding the proper room, I waited until my number was called, then entered. I felt unsure of myself, and the thin man of about 60 standing in the center of the room did nothing to alleviate my stress. He gazed sternly at me, waiting for me to speak.

"Good afternoon," I said. "Are you the gentleman I need to see about obtaining a visa?"

"Why do you speak in English?" he answered.

"I'm sorry Mr. ..." I said, pausing for him to fill in the blank.

"Filzek," he answered.

"I don't know German," I stated. "I arrived in Germany only two weeks ago. I assumed, because of your position, you knew English."

Mr. Filzek motioned for me to come to his desk and be seated. As he questioned me, I realized he did not have an easy job, handling so many different people. At times it would be difficult for him even to know who was telling the truth.

Finally, his questioning complete, Mr. Filzek said curtly, "Well, priest, this will take about three months to be approved."

I thanked him and left.

A few days later, I purchased a 7-year-old green Audi that seemed to be in good repair. I understood I could not purchase a vehicle until I had my residence visa, but the salesman assured me it was no problem in Germany to purchase one beforehand. He explained all I had to do was take the papers that showed I had paid for the car to the building on Mainzer Landstrasse. "There you will be given permission to purchase a license tag," he said.

So once again I found myself in the immigration office. Finally, after another long wait, my number was called and I once again entered Mr. Filzek's office.

"Mr. Filzek," I said, "I've purchased a car and here are the sales papers. I believe I need your approval so I can obtain a license tag."

"I cannot approve that," Mr. Filzek replied, his voice sounding somewhat irritated. "You can't purchase a car until you have your residence visa. That takes three months to clear, as I told you earlier."

"But the salesman said it wouldn't be a problem to get approval for the car," I stated.

"He just wanted to sell you a car," Mr. Filzek replied.

"I'm sorry," I said, feeling that I had unintentionally put Mr. Filzek on the spot. "I don't want to create a problem for you."

Mr. Filzek's expression did not change and I sat quietly. After a long pause, he reached for my file and asked for my passport. Selecting the proper stamp on his desk, he stamped in a temporary residence visa in my passport and signed it. Even though he had the authority, I sensed this was an unusual event.

"All right," he said. "Now go finish your paperwork on the car."

"Thank you very much," I replied.

Finding an apartment so quickly wasn't the only dead bolt door that had been opened. Being able to purchase a car within those first 30 days was another.

God must have a special work for us here before we return to Pakistan, I reasoned.

Down on the street, as I waited to catch a tram, I thought about Mr. Filzek. Underneath his rough, frank exterior, I believed I had detected a soft heart.

Perhaps there are things I don't understand about Germans like Mr. Filzek, I thought.

About a month later I felt an urge to return to Mr. Filzek's office. I waited an hour before my number was called. Again

I faced Mr. Filzek, noticing he was wearing the same gray sweater.

"All right," he said crisply, not even bothering to raise his eyes from his desk. "What is your problem this time?"

"I don't have a problem, Mr. Filzek," I answered. "I just came to see how you are doing."

He stopped working, sat up straighter in his swivel chair, and said, "What?"

"Please pardon me for interrupting," I stated, "but I just came to see how you are doing."

"Do you mean to tell me you waited for more than an hour just to come in here and ask me how I am doing?" he said, looking at me with a tinge of suspicion.

"That's right, Mr. Filzek," I answered. "How are you doing? You don't seem to have a very easy job."

Perplexed and unsmiling, Mr. Filzek leaned way back in his chair, smoothed his slick, graying hair, and studied me more closely. Finally he responded. "You're right," he said. "Do you realize my assistant and I are in charge of 8,000 cases?" He pointed to numerous circular files to his left and right. Then standing up he asked, "Would you like a cup of coffee?"

"If you'll have one with me," I replied.

"Tell me, Mr. Leatherberry, do you think there is any hope for this world?" he asked as he poured two cups of coffee. Without waiting for a reply, he handed a cup to me and continued, "Don't you think things are getting worse every day? Do you think there is hope for an old man like me?"

Though his questions could be interpreted as rhetorical, they sounded very sincere—as though he had previously given them serious thought.

"Mr. Filzek, you're right," I responded. "The world is getting worse every day. A person has to be blind not to realize that. But there is hope in this world, and for you, because of the Lord Jesus Christ."

"Aach! Don't talk to me about church," he said in a loud voice. "I haven't gone for years."

Acting upon his forthrightness, I said, "Mr. Filzek, I'm not talking to you about going to church. I'm talking about knowing Christ and the peace and hope He gives."

Our discussion continued for some time and I began to worry about the others who were waiting outside Mr. Filzek's door. However, he seemed to be in no hurry, so I stayed awhile longer. When I finally excused myself, Mr. Filzek smiled warmly and shook my hand. He invited me to telephone him so we could arrange a visit at his home. This was indeed a very gracious act since he had known me for such a short time.

My feet wanted to dance down the street as I left the plain, bureaucratic-looking building. Though the sun wasn't shining and it was chilly and rainy, my heart felt warm and sunny. I had made a friend. How grateful I was I had obeyed the urging I had received during my time of prayer.

Dead bolt doors had once again swung open.

What thrilled me even more was the doors were not slowly creaking open; they were swiftly and in a timely fashion opening wide. Far more important than getting an apartment or obtaining permission to drive the Audi was the fact Mr. Filzek had opened the heaviest of all doors to me—the door to his heart.

14

I WILL TELL THEM

Thoughts about our upcoming conversational English classes for Afghans filled my mind.

"Let's use the living room as one classroom and one of our bedrooms for the other," Julie suggested, surveying our apartment.

We calculated we could handle a maximum of 40 students in our four, 50-minute classes each morning. We would conduct these classes five days each week. Julie would teach four or five women in each class in the living room, and I would teach four or five men in each class in the other room.

When we told Jamil about our plans, he helped us in every way. The other Afghans trusted Jamil, so we were grateful when he recommended our classes to them. Jamil helped us screen and interview potential students.

During the interview, Julie and I explained we were Americans supported by the church to assist them in their transition to the United States. This was a concept the Afghans understood since many of them were under church sponsorship to go to the U.S.

"If you have not applied for United States entry, you should be learning German," we said to them. "But if you are planning on going to the States, we are here to provide this service for you. We want to help you in any way we can."

Soon the openings for our 40 students had been filled. Now I faced another challenge. How was I going to explain to the German apartment manager that 40 Afghans would be coming to his apartment complex every morning, five days a week? Not only was such a thing universally frowned upon, but it was usually forbidden. Some apartment managers even had the authority to refuse specific persons from visiting another individual's apartment. I needed another miracle.

I telephoned my good German friend Karl, who lived in Stuttgart, many miles from Frankfurt. I had known Karl when we lived in Afghanistan. During our telephone conversation I explained my situation to him.

"You've got a problem for sure, David," Karl said. "What makes you think any apartment manager in Germany is going to permit 40 students to come to your apartment for classes?"

"I admit this is a little unusual, Karl," I said, understating the situation. "However, this is not a formal school. I am not charging fees, I'm paying the rent, and these students are all my guests."

My reasoning was completely unconvincing to my friend, but I ventured on.

"Karl, since I can only say hello and good-bye in German, I would like for you to speak to the *hausmeister* on my behalf," I told him. "Could you please explain to him what I plan to do so he will understand what is happening? I'll be glad to answer any of his questions."

Complete silence. It seemed as if a full minute passed before Karl replied, "I see what you mean, David. But you don't understand the German mind-set. Germans are private people, especially in their homes. Any *hausmeister* would immediately envision people stomping in and

going out at all hours. He would refuse your request on
the spot."

"I understand, Karl, but will you at least try?"

"Yes, David," Karl replied quietly.

I knew Karl would gladly do it for me, but I also knew
he sensed the futility of what I was trying to do.

"Thanks," I said. "Let's pray, then I'll get the apartment
manager and call you back."

We had a short word of prayer.

I found the manager, brought him to my apartment,
then called Karl. Handing the phone to the manager, I
waited as he spoke to my friend. I carefully watched his
face for a clue to his response. I was unable to read anything. Finally he returned the phone to me.

"Hello, Karl," I said. "How did it go?"

Karl began laughing, "David, this is incredible. I can
hardly believe it. He said it's a wonderful idea for you to
teach Afghans English. He says if there is anything at all
he can do to help you, please let him know. He wants to
know if you need anything. He only asks that the students
come and go quietly, not linger in the hallways, or drop
papers. He said his wife was a refugee from East Germany
and he understands."

I wanted to shout "Praise the Lord!" but I maintained
my composure and thanked Karl. The *hausmeister*
grinned and I vigorously shook his hand and smiled so
hard my face hurt. In pantomime, he raised his hand as if
drinking a beer and motioned me to follow him. I knew
he was trying to be hospitable by offering me a drink in
his apartment, but I politely refused because, due to my
personal conviction, I do not drink alcohol. Wondering how I could ever explain to this kind German man
why I didn't drink, I smiled again, trying to convey my

gratefulness to him. He smiled back, raised his eyebrows, shrugged his shoulders, and left.

I later discovered 10 days before we rented the apartment he had become the new *hausmeister*. The previous one had been staunchly prejudiced against foreigners. Was it coincidental that the change had been made at that time? I hardly think so. Thanks to the wonderful cooperation of the new *hausmeister*, it would be no problem for the Afghans to come to our apartment.

As we established the language school we were very concerned about building trust between ourselves and our students. Though Jamil's honorable reputation and recommendation of us paved the way for our initial acceptance by the Afghans, that in itself was not sufficient. Julie and I had to prove ourselves as trustworthy persons. But how?

Most of the Afghan refugees had been taken advantage of in various ways by a number of people, so they were disinclined to trust strangers. Why should they trust us? Would they wonder what we wanted?

I took this problem to the Lord in prayer. "Lord, how can they know that Julie and I are reliable? How can they even know we are for real ... that we want to help, not hurt? We want to lift up, not tear down. I wouldn't blame them for not trusting us."

The answer the Lord brought so clearly to my mind was almost too simple to believe: *I'll tell them you are for real.*

Now that was an answer I couldn't have come up with. The Afghans would hear no voice; they simply would sense we could be trusted. God would verify our credentials of honest love. Our fivefold responsibility was to be prayerful and faithful to God, to be sensitive to the deep hurts of the Afghans, to give ourselves to them, to be conscientious teachers, and to be genuinely sincere. God would do the rest.

From that time on I relaxed and ceased worrying about being misunderstood.

With classes starting soon, Julie and I busied ourselves by preparing lesson plans for the beginners and for the more advanced. We tried to find good English-as-a-Second-Language textbooks to use, but were disappointed after reviewing several. The teaching principles were excellent, but the content was often contrary to Afghan culture, as well as our own convictions. We were not interested in teaching such things as how to get your palms read or how to buy whiskey.

Convinced we should prepare our own lessons, we began writing. It was more work than we had anticipated. Julie wrote the beginning course and I wrote the others. We based our lessons on principles we had learned from the different textbooks we had reviewed. We created our own stories and conversational situations we felt would be most helpful to the Afghans. Then we made audiotapes to go with the lessons.

Our mini-school began in April 1981 with 40 students who were eager to learn. Classes were enjoyable for Julie and me, and our students seemed devoted to them. The first sessions sailed along and we settled into a comfortable routine.

It wasn't long before our students knew and trusted us as God had promised. The better acquainted we became with them, the more we realized what competent and capable people we were teaching. Businessmen, teachers, lawyers, housewives, doctors, officials, as well as high school and university students made up our class rosters.

Many of them kindly invited us to their small hotel

rooms for Afghan meals. During these times together they shared with us tragic stories of betrayals, pursuits, persecutions, imprisonments, tortures, executions, and narrow escapes. Their unfortunate experiences were usually caused by their refusal to cooperate with the communist party or to be reeducated. Therefore, they were considered reactionaries—a cancer for society to eradicate.

Theirs was a grim choice indeed: conform or suffer the consequences. Hundreds, perhaps thousands, of their fellow countrymen were eliminated, and tens of thousands fled Afghanistan to save their lives.

Most of the refugees had suffered the loss of houses and property, but their greatest pain was caused by having to leave family members and friends in their homeland.

Julie and I would listen intently to their stories of grief and heartache. In some ways, it wasn't hard to put ourselves in their shoes, for we had walked down many of their former streets. Often we knew exactly where they had lived or the location of their neighborhoods. We could easily visualize their homes and way of life before the radical disruption reduced them to standing in line at a German social welfare office.

Many people would not consider these Afghans refugees, for they were well dressed and educated—they did not fit the refugee stereotype. Yet refugees they were. They were displaced—subjected to the same mental, psychological, and emotional trauma all refugees experience. They struggled to cope with such guilt-ridden questions as, "Why was my life spared when friends or family members were not?" or "Why was I fortunate enough to escape when others were unable to do so?"

One of our students, Nadir, was a medical student from Kabul University. Along with a fellow student named

Toryawli, he had been arrested by soldiers for participating in a demonstration against the communist regime. They were taken to a prison by truck and separately interrogated. Alone, in his barren cell, Nadir heard Toryawli scream from a room down the hall. The communists were prodding him with electric shocks and pulling out his fingernails and toenails.

"Stop it!" Nadir yelled to the unknown assailants.

When the screaming finally did stop, Nadir sat on the small, hard cot, pushed his black hair back with both hands, and found himself remembering how he and Toryawli had walked to grade school together in Shari Now and shared dreams of attending the prestigious Hibibiya High School. He had teased his friend about med school saying, "I didn't make it. You are going to med school alone." But of course they went together; they did everything together.

Later that night, Toryawli and five other prisoners were taken outside, placed against the wall, and gunned down with machine guns. In his dark cell, the rapid clip of the gunfire brought Nadir to his feet. Grasping the prison bars, he shouted, "No! No!" Then he put his forehead against the cold steel and wept. In his heart, he knew his beloved companion was dead.

Three days later, untouched and without any explanation, Nadir was released. An undeniable guilt for simply being alive seared his conscience like a branding iron.

Why had he been set free? Who would believe he had not cooperated with the communists or betrayed his friend? These thoughts flooded his mind.

Nadir's family feared for his life, suspecting he would be rearrested at any time as many others had. Persuaded by his father to escape to Pakistan, he said a sorrowful farewell to his elderly parents and his three sisters and their young children. He then took a rickety bus to Kandahar where he stayed hidden for a week in his uncle's home. During that time arrangements were made with a guide to take him the long way around through the desert to Pakistan.

After paying an exorbitant price, Nadir and a family with three teenage boys followed the guide to Pakistan. They traveled on foot at night. From there, he made his way to Germany and into my class.

When he finished telling me his story one afternoon in our apartment, his face was damp with tears.

"Why was my life spared and not my friend's?" he asked.

We sat in silence. Any attempt to answer would have been insensitive and unworthy of my young friend's pain.

As our Afghan students shared their stories, our admiration for their courage and respect for their dignity deepened. We walked softly among them, learning to understand them and trying to pour God's healing oil on their emotional wounds. I wanted to shout to the world to be loving with them. They were not just refugees; they were individuals who had feelings just like ours.

The first 13-week session ended in early July. Julie and I continued to prepare lessons for the next session, all the while helping our Afghan friends sort out the bureaucratic maze and red tape they encountered seeking refugee papers for the United States.

The need for our classes was so great Julie and I decided we should teach twice as many students as we had in the first session. I began searching for larger quarters to accommodate those on our waiting list.

I made some inquiries at institutions that might have large classrooms and learned such space was almost impossible to rent. There seemed to be no way of obtaining what we needed, so I asked God for a solution.

About halfway between our apartment and the hotel where many of the Afghan families lived, I noticed several large stately buildings. I'd assumed they were government buildings. Upon inquiry, I learned they belonged to a *fachhochschule* (a technical college).

On a Tuesday in August I looked out of our apartment window at downtown Frankfurt and prayed, "I need classrooms, Lord. What shall I do?"

The answer was so specific, it startled me.

David, on Thursday, at 11 o'clock in the morning, if you will go to the office building of the fachhochschule *you will find a man who has the authority to rent you two classrooms. He will be completely sympathetic.*

The curious thing about this whole idea was that most of Frankfurt, including all the schools, was on vacation. Even knowing this, I could hardly wait for Thursday.

I arrived outside the office building just before 11 on Thursday morning and waited. At exactly 11 o'clock, I walked up a short flight of stairs and went inside.

This is going to be interesting, I thought. *I wonder what kind of man I will meet.*

No one was in the large hallway, so I stood with my hands in my pockets. After a while, I began to feel a little foolish. Then a thought crossed my mind that comforted me some: *If this doesn't work out, at least no one will know about it.* At the same time, I was puzzled because I was sure I had heard from God.

The brisk click of a woman's shoes on the marble floor caught my attention. I turned my head to see a middle-aged, bespectacled woman with short, slightly graying hair approach the copy machine in the hall. She pushed up her gold, wire-rimmed glasses, gave me a quick smile of acknowledgment, put a paper on the glass, and started the machine. When she finished, she walked over and began to talk to me in German.

As politely as I could, I interrupted her with, "I'm sorry, I don't speak German."

She studied me thoughtfully, then suddenly motioned for me to follow her.

Down the hall, outside of one of the offices, she put both hands up about shoulder high and then quickly brought them down about four inches. I interpreted this nonverbal sign as "Stop and wait." I obeyed and she disappeared into the office.

After two or three minutes, a man in his late thirties came out. He had bright blue eyes and, though dressed in slacks and shirt, he gave an impression of professional confidence. Shaking my hand he greeted me in English, invited me into his office, and kindly asked, "How may I help you, sir?"

After I had explained what I needed, he asked me several questions in perfect English about my motivation, how long I needed the space, and how many persons would be involved.

After listening to my answers, he remarked, "This is really interesting. Here's an American in Germany who wants to teach Afghans English. I think it's unusual but a very kind, generous thing you are doing. I believe I can help you. However, you will have to verify your sponsorship."

"Guess who I just met?" I exclaimed to Julie when I

returned home. "Peter Gussmann, vice chancellor of the college."

I provided the necessary proof to Mr. Gussmann and he granted us two classrooms from four p.m. to eight p.m., five days a week for 12 weeks. All utilities and maintenance costs were included in the minimal fee.

A couple of weeks later I stopped by Mr. Gussmann's office. During my visit he stated, "One thing I don't understand. How did you know to come and see me? No one else in Frankfurt would have rented you classrooms."

"This is going to sound a little different," I replied. Then I told him of my experience in prayer and my obedience.

Pushing himself back from the table he said thoughtfully, "Hmmm, that's a little different all right. That's outside my experience."

At my request, the vice chancellor personally addressed our students in class and said he was happy to have them on campus. One of the older Afghans responded on behalf of the students by thanking Mr. Gussmann. An interesting cross-cultural difference surfaced during the dialogue. Germans usually say thanks once and mean it. Afghans, however, will offer gratitude several times, responding to "You're welcome," with "Thank you," followed by a "You're entirely welcome," followed by another "Thank you." The vice chancellor seemed both amused and impressed by the Afghans' sincere appreciation.

After that, Peter Gussmann and his wife, Irlis, befriended us and invited Julie and me to their home.

Guido Braun, a rotund man in his early fifties, often watched me zip into his quick-print shop right before class to make copies of our English lessons on two machines simultaneously. He stood behind the counter, watching my nervous race-in-race-out behavior with amusement.

One day I turned from my work as I heard his infectious laugh. He said, "Leatherberry, you are a funny guy. You charge into my shop all the time, running around like a chicken with your head cut off. But you really have peace."

Thank You, Lord, I thought.

Another time, I had just run off a bunch of papers, hardly taking time to say hello before hurrying out the door. Guido stepped out after me and stood on the top step watching me go.

Partway down the block I turned around and started back toward him. I was about to speak when he threw up his hands and stopped me with, "I know, Dave. I know. There's no one more important to God than me and He has a beautiful plan for my life!"

I smiled at what he was saying. Often I had told Guido that truth as I left the shop; now he tossed my words back at me.

"Guido," I responded, "you are absolutely right. I'm excited about your life and God's fantastic plan for you. Just give Him a chance, Guido, just a chance."

He nodded.

How I wanted to pull him into the kingdom of God. As I began to make my way to class once again, I asked God to let it happen soon. I considered Guido to be defenseless against my prayers.

There were times when I would drop in at Guido's shop just to chat with him. When this happened we would launch into a philosophical debate that he loved, for he was very well read and spoke several languages. I was impressed with his English, which he spoke without accent. He tried to disprove my arguments for God's existence, yet I had the feeling he was forcing me to strengthen my position so he might fully consider it for himself.

Guido had a hard time explaining a person like me to himself. It didn't take him long to realize perhaps I was more than a naive, enthusiastic American who had the audacity to say he carried on informal conversations with God.

Our busy schedule of classes never felt like work, and our eager anticipation continued from week to week. Steadily the Afghans were acquiring English and becoming our good friends.

In the midst of it all, Julie and I were happy.

15

HIDDEN HUNGER

Lila Akbare was a slender Afghan teenager. Her soft brown hair parted in the middle, then fell straight down her back and away from her round pleasant face. In English class Julie found Lila to be self-confident, yet humble. She had a sincere and unshakable faith in the reality of God. Lila's gifts were soon obvious to us. With her intense desire to help her own people, we felt certain she would reach her goal of becoming a medical doctor.

When she invited Julie and me to dinner we accepted with pleasure.

The tantalizing aroma of Afghan food in the hotel hallway reached us long before we reached the Akbare family's room. Lila's father warmly greeted and welcomed us at the door. Then we were introduced to several other members of this rather large family. Immediately their genuine acceptance, which went beyond normal politeness, made us feel right at home. Over tea we exchanged information regarding our families and talked about our common interests concerning Afghanistan.

Shortly after dinner, Mr. Akbare turned the conversation to a discussion about Almighty God. My statement that I not only believed wholeheartedly in God but that He was the center of my life thoroughly delighted him.

Mr. Akbare, an open-minded man who was thirsty for God, had earned an advanced degree in science from a

European university. He respected the Bible as a holy book and viewed Jesus as a great prophet. In a sensitive manner, he quizzed me about differences in our beliefs.

I appreciated the respect I received from Mr. Akbare—the same respect I have always enjoyed with Muslims—and my mind formed a prayer as he was forming questions. *Lord, let me be forthright in sharing, but always in love, taking the apostle Peter's words to heart to* "... *always be prepared to give an answer to everyone who asks you to give the reason for the hope that you have. But do this with gentleness and respect*" (1 Peter 3:15).

Mr. Akbare's face was serious when he asked, "Mr. David, it seems you believe in three gods while we believe in one. Is this not true?"

In my mind I struggled to answer in a way that would make sense to him. I pressed my lips together and pondered hard. Long before this moment occurred, I had faced the issue of the wholeness of God through the Trinity. It had never been an easy issue for me. Mr. Akbare waited patiently for me to organize my thoughts.

"Mr. Akbare," I finally replied, "I do not believe in three gods. This I can assure you. Like you, I believe in one eternal, Almighty God. The Holy Bible teaches, 'The Lord our God, the Lord is one' (Deuteronomy 6:4)."

I detected a pleasant smile on his face.

Was this a smile of relief or gladness? Unable to answer the question, I continued. "I cannot fully comprehend or explain God. If I could, He would not be God. But I do know what God has revealed about himself in the Holy Bible."

As Mr. Akbare nodded his head, I went on: "I believe in the unity of God, but the Holy Bible reveals that it's a complex unity. For within God there are three personalities in one, and one in three personalities."

"But, Mr. David, how can that be?" my friend earnestly questioned.

"Mr. Akbare, perhaps this will give us a hint at how it can be. You have a mind, body, and spirit, yet you are one. How can that be? Time consists of past, present, and future, yet time is one. The atom, the smallest particle of matter, is composed of protons, electrons, and neutrons, yet the atom is one. How can that be?"

"Hmmm," Mr. Akbare said, pursing his lips.

Our conversation began to include other family members and continued into the night as we sipped tea.

A few days later, Julie answered the phone. It was Lila calling to make a request. "Would you mind if my father, my sister, and I stopped by for a visit some afternoon?" she asked. She explained her father had been considering our discussion and further questions had arisen in his mind.

"We would be happy for you to come by," Julie told her.

A couple of days later our doorbell rang. We invited the Akbares in, put some nuts and candies out to have with our tea, and began to talk. It was a good discussion that lasted about two hours.

Mr. Akbare said, "Mr. David, really we believe alike in many ways. Different roads lead to God."

I thought a moment, then ventured, "Mr. Akbare, would you agree with me the real issue is not what man thinks is the way to God, but what is God's way to God?"

The expression on his face told me that this was a new thought.

"Yes, Mr. David, that is true," he answered. "But, Mr. David, how do we know what is God's way to God? I have been taught a certain way all of my life. How do I know which is God's way? Is it the way I have been taught or the way you say?"

Lila leaned forward on the edge of the couch with an earnest expression. "How do we really know the truth?" she asked.

These Afghan friends touched my heart with such pure honesty. A deep sigh escaped my lips. Looking at Mr. Akbare and then at Lila, I finally said, "I don't know what to say to you except to tell you to ask God himself to show you which way is His path to Him. You must know from Him for yourself."

They both nodded slowly as I spoke, intent on every word I said.

I continued, "But, please remember that if you ask God which way is His, you may discover it is different than you think. It may cost you a lot. Are you prepared to follow His way whatever that cost may be?"

I did not expect an answer, but I could see that to Lila and Mr. Akbare this idea made sense. Lila turned to her younger sister and carefully translated what was said.

By this time, it was getting late and our guests had to leave. They finished their tea and we walked the few steps to the elevator with them where we said good-bye.

Alone in our apartment, yet still feeling the glow of those beautiful, inquiring people, we felt both happy and frustrated at what had just taken place. God's presence at that time was, however, very reassuring.

"Lord," I prayed, "please do what I cannot do. Reveal yourself to my friends who long to know the truth. Please satisfy the hidden hunger in their hearts."

Wali was another one of our students who was

immediately likable. Whether it was because of his hearty laughter, his midrange chuckle, or his infectious smile, I couldn't say. All I knew was that each day I looked forward to Wali's arrival in class where he struggled to learn English.

He had a tendency to put his English in reverse order and mix tenses, which always worried him. "Yesterday to store I gone," he'd say.

I liked the way Wali allowed himself to laugh as he tried so hard to learn. Remembering my own struggle with Pushtu, I encouraged him often. "You can learn English. Don't give up," I told him over and over. At home I prayed God would help him with his new language.

Wali's ready smile and pleasant way did not mean he was without difficulties. At 30 years of age he had left his homeland. Part of his family was still there, some of whom were in prison. He was a refugee in a strange land, wrestling with a new language, and endeavoring to take care of his family on a very limited budget.

His wife, Habiba, was a modest, polite, well-mannered woman with short hair, a slightly plump look, and, as Julie said, beautiful eyes. Habiba was always thoughtful and eager to make you comfortable. She too was familiar with grief. Her teenage brother had been shot to death by a Soviet soldier.

Habiba was busy even when it wasn't necessary, moving about with an ever-present appearance of strain. We had been told she cried excessively during the night. This made Julie wonder if she was close to a nervous breakdown. Like many of the Afghan women in Germany, Habiba longed to hear news from the rest of her family in Afghanistan, but censored letters gave little information.

Sometimes at night, Wali would read a story from the

New Testament to his troubled wife. "This seems to help her sleep," he told me.

During one of my visits to his room he held the New Testament up with both hands and said, "I never knew what was inside this Book. It's beautiful. All those stories of Jesus healing sick people and all those miracles He did. Jesus loved people."

Wali told me of his desire to have a clean heart, but he felt it could not be possible. I could see in his eyes the deep longing of his heart to be pure and holy before the perfect God.

"It's not impossible to be pure before God, Wali," I said to him.

He looked at me as if I were naive and did not understand. Then raising his voice a little, he asked, "How, Mr. David, can that possibly be?"

"We cannot make ourselves pure or forgive ourselves of sin," I replied. "No matter how hard I try, I cannot do enough good things to earn my way to heaven."

Wali looked very disappointed. I only seemed to verify what he already felt in his heart to be true.

Then I went on. "Wali, God loves us. Yet to truly love us, He must be truly just. He must punish our sin."

He interrupted, "But, Mr. David, what can we do? We are all guilty before God."

I had to contain my amazement of his grasp of that simple fact that eludes so many people the world over. We're not okay. We're all guilty of sin. None of us can earn eternal life. It is only by God's grace we can be reconciled to Him.

Thinking about this I said, "Wali, that's why I'm so thankful to the Lord Jesus Christ. He was pure and perfect, yet He took the punishment I deserve by His voluntary sacrifice on the cross for me. That makes me acceptable before God."

When hearing this idea for the first time, it is difficult for most people to respond immediately. As Wali paused, I thought about the disaster in his homeland. "If soldiers with machine guns knocked on your door at midnight to take you away to torture and execute you," I said, "but I stepped in and insisted they take me instead, would you be grateful to me?"

"Certainly, Mr. David. Certainly," he replied.

Looking directly at him I said, "Wali, I want you to know something. I would really do that for you."

Deep emotion, for which I was not prepared, swept through him. "Thank you, Mr. David. I know you would," he responded, his eyes moistening.

"That is why I love the Lord Jesus Christ," I said. "He actually took our place, Wali. No one else did that for me. Only Christ could. When I asked Him to forgive me, He did. I became pure in the eyes of God because of Christ's suffering for me."

There was no response to my words, only a long silence. Then I continued, "Wali, Jesus purchased eternal life for us with His sacrifice. Now He offers eternal life to us as a free gift. But it's our choice whether or not we accept it. We should not allow ourselves to refuse it because of our pride."

He looked at the floor as if contemplating a decision. Then he lifted his head, raised his eyebrows slightly, and questioned, "How is that done, Mr. David?"

"You like to take long walks by the river, don't you?" I asked. Then, without waiting for him to answer, I continued, "So do I. Often I take walks by myself just to talk with the Lord Jesus Christ."

Feeling Wali's eyes intent on my face, I said, "May I suggest that someday soon you take an unhurried walk by yourself? Just start talking with the Lord Jesus, for He is a living person who rose from the dead. You can be informal in your speech, but talk reverently with Him in your own words. He is there."

Wali showed no nervousness, fear, or disbelief in what I was relating to him.

"Thank Him," I said, "for dying on the cross for your sins. Thank Him for personally loving you. Ask Him to forgive all your sins and to come into your life—to give you eternal life. Then you will experience His peace and His presence."

The next day I walked along the tree-lined River Main to have fellowship with the Lord Jesus. I praised and thanked the God of the universe who would someday allow me to join Him forever. I stopped and admired God's handiwork evidenced by the delicately colored, fragrant flowers along my way.

Then I remembered my conversation with Wali and I wondered if he was walking too.

16

LIGHT IN THE FACE OF LOGIC

From our balcony we could see downtown Frankfurt as well as the rooftops of the residential area. I liked to stand at the window, look out over Frankfurt, and pray for the city.

Beyond the edge of the city and parallel to our apartment, jets followed their flight pattern to land at the Frankfurt International Airport. Julie and I often watched the jets, straining our eyes to catch a glimpse of the various airline markings on the tails, wondering where they were coming from. Pakistan maybe.

"I'd sure like to be on one of those flights heading for Peshawar or Kabul," I would say wistfully to Julie quite often.

Like the wool in a good Afghan carpet, several experiences with the Lord were woven into our 12-month stay in Germany. The instructions and directions coming out of those experiences were lessons in living as followers of Christ. My strongest desire was to be submissive to God and please Him—even when I didn't understand how His directions would work out.

The first of these directions came to me one day in April 1981, hardly a month after our arrival in Frankfurt.

We had purchased a car, moved into our apartment, and

had our English classes scheduled. As I stood looking at the city from our balcony window that day, I talked to the Lord, praying about personal concerns and mentioning my family. I was not praying for Afghanistan as I usually did.

As I prayed I paused for a second, and to my great surprise these words swiftly and forcibly entered my consciousness just as clearly as if they had been spoken: *David, I'm sending you back to Kabul, Afghanistan.*

The very idea had me nearly reeling.

"God, that's impossible," I said. "You and I have been there. We know the situation. They are never going to give a visa to me due to the fact I'm an American. The Soviets are in charge of Kabul."

My explanation apparently did not impress God, because as powerfully and as clearly as before I heard once again: *David, I'm sending you back to Kabul, Afghanistan. I have already given the command for those visas to be issued to you.*

Upon hearing those words I responded, "Lord, this does not appear to be wise. There are 20,000 Afghans here, that same number in New Delhi, and more than 2 million in Pakistan. Why do You want to send me to a restricted place where I will hardly be able to talk to people?"

Then I remembered the assurance of our return to Afghanistan I had received when we departed from Peshawar. Now I felt a deep sense of harmony that surpassed everything else. God's plan for us seemed impossible, illogical, impractical, and unthinkable. But I couldn't wait to tell Julie that we were going back to Kabul.

Far better than anyone else, Julie knows how imperfect I am, yet she has confidence in me. It wasn't that she felt I couldn't make a mistake in hearing from God, for there were times when I had felt sure, yet was mistaken.

Because Julie and I knew the vital importance of confirmation, I wrote letters to the Assemblies of God leaders to whom we were directly responsible requesting permission to seek a way to return to Afghanistan. I have high regard for these men of faith and experience, so when they granted the requested permission Julie and I felt we had received the first confirmation we needed.

Next I wrote to Bill Thompson, the head of an international medical team in Kabul, asking him to place an application with the Afghan government requesting I be granted a visa to teach English to Afghan doctors. He wrote back asking that I send him our passport numbers as soon as possible. These numbers were required for the visa applications.

We needed to obtain new passports, but I was reluctant to approach the American Consulate in Frankfurt because my previous experiences with the consulate had not been positive. I considered going to the American Embassy in Bonn for new passports, but wondered how I could explain why I hadn't gone to the consulate in Frankfurt where I lived.

After prayer, Julie and I both felt we should go to Bonn, so we made plans to go the next day.

When it came time to leave the next morning, I was reluctant—afraid it wouldn't work.

Julie tried to assure me. "David," she said, "I'm sure we are to go to Bonn today."

"No," I said. "Let's take a break and go see John and Anita Koeshall in Munich." To reach them would require several hours by car.

"Okay," Julie said. "But I still think we should go to Bonn."

Upon reaching Munich we hit a snowstorm that caused a gigantic traffic jam. After getting lost for over an hour, we finally got to the Koeshalls'. Neither one of them was feeling well, and since we were tired from the drive we all agreed to turn in early that night.

How foolish to have made this trip, I thought as I settled myself in bed.

About three in the morning, I awoke and became fully aware of God's presence. He asked, *David, what are you doing in Munich? I instructed you to go to Bonn.*

I had disobeyed the Lord, and now I didn't see a way out of the problem I had created. It would be another 30 days before I could go to Bonn.

I said, "I'm sorry, Lord."

The next day we returned to Frankfurt. As we made our way home, I apologized to my wife.

"It's okay. I feel bad about the lost time, but we'll work it out," she said smiling.

Back in Frankfurt, I still felt uneasy regarding Bonn. Then one night I dreamed I was in an American Embassy and a very kind official kept saying, "Now, Mr. Leatherberry, is there anything else I can do for you? I'll be glad to do whatever I can."

Puzzled, I wondered why this man was being so good to me. After I awakened, this clear statement came to me: *David, I want you to remember this; I have some of My men in such places.*

"Yes, Lord," I humbly replied. Corrected, I determined not to forget what the Lord had communicated to me.

A month later we were on the 5:30 a.m. train headed for Bonn. The sleek train sped smoothly along and by midmorning, right on time, we pulled into the station.

A cab delivered us across town to the large, impressive

marble embassy. We breathed a prayer and walked inside to the passport section where a polite American consul worker soon called us to the window. Through the glass, he asked if he could help us.

I explained to him we needed new passports. Though he was greatly surprised that we wanted to go into war-torn Afghanistan, I assured him we were going.

"Please fill out these forms over at the table," he said, slipping the papers through the small opening under the glass window. "Then return them to me. It should only take a few minutes then to issue the new passports to you." His kindness to us was just like the man in the dream.

Julie and I followed his instructions, returned the forms, and thanked him.

Within a few minutes, his secretary called us. She had the new passports in her hand.

"Oh," she said, "I see that you live in Frankfurt."

My thoughts raced. I knew this would cause a problem. Now what am I going to say? Impulsively I replied, "Well, sometimes in the East it can be more helpful if our passports are issued from a capital city such as Bonn."

That is absolutely correct, I thought. Now why hadn't I thought of that before?

"Mr. Leatherberry," she said without judgment, "we don't care where you get your passports."

Feeling like children who unexpectedly had received new toys, we emerged from the American Embassy with our new passports. As we stood alone, waiting for the bus to take us back to the train station, Julie bubbled over with praise. With joy she sang, "The steadfast love of the Lord never ceases. His mercies never come to an end. They are new every morning, new every morning. Great is Thy faithfulness."

Once again we were learning to place our trust totally in the Lord and to follow through on whatever He said.

On the train back to Frankfurt, I peered out the window thinking, *Surely God's ways are above ours just as the prophet Isaiah said.* My thoughts wandered back to 1977, our second year in Kabul. At that time I had longed to sit down and have a heart-to-heart talk with any one of my close friends in the United States who had known me over the years, but that was not possible. However, I needed to unburden my mind, to receive counsel on my problems.

A few nights later, I had a dream. In the dream, a pastor-friend from my teenage years came to the door of my house in Kabul. I welcomed him in and we sat together for tea. The sun shone brightly as we spent the afternoon in heart-to-heart conversation. He helped me understand many things, and I received answers to many of my questions.

I awoke from the dream feeling completely relaxed and my mind greatly relieved. The psychological and emotional refreshing was the same as if the experience had actually happened.

I had never read or heard of any such thing happening, but I couldn't think of anything in the Bible that contradicted such an experience. I knew there were times when God guided people through dreams, but I also knew such experiences were never to take precedence over the Bible.

The train back to Frankfurt rolled on with its rhythmic clacking. I was learning I shouldn't try to put my limitations on God's creative guidance.

Back in Frankfurt, the weeks rolled by and the time for

our return to our beloved land came swiftly. Even though we were excited about going back to the nation of our calling, parting from those in Frankfurt who had become such close friends would not be without its usual pain—a pain we would never get used to.

17

"NOW WHO'S GOING TO TELL US WE'RE GOING TO MAKE IT?"

As soon as word was out we were leaving Germany for Asia, our Afghan friends started inviting us to their homes for visits and meals.

One such family was headed by Merwis, a middle-aged man from Kabul. I liked this proud man. He was polite, yet he was also straightforward enough to question me or even correct me if I mispronounced a word in the advanced English class he attended. Though I hadn't met him before coming to Germany, he remembered seeing my name on a purchase order at the private company he had worked for in Kabul. In Frankfurt, our friendship had grown and blossomed.

"Come have a farewell lunch with us," Merwis suggested. "Mina wants to prepare something special for you."

When we arrived at his home, we found that his lovely wife, Mina, had prepared one of my favorite Asian dishes, *bulane*. *Bulane* is flat, fried dough, with a potato-onion filling that is eaten with yogurt. I was always amazed at the way Afghan women could cook such a wide variety of delicious foods from scratch with such limited facilities in their cramped refugee hotel rooms—rooms so unlike their former homes in Kabul.

When the meal was finished, we had the customary tea. Julie and Mina sat together, looking at family photograph albums. When Julie came to the end of an album, a loose picture fell to the floor and she picked it up.

"Where did you get this picture, Mina?" she exclaimed.

"It came only recently from my father. That is why it isn't permanently in the album yet," Mina replied.

"David," Julie said, trying to conceal her excitement. "Look at this picture taken by Mina's father."

Puzzled, I looked first at her, then at the photo. It was an almost perfect shot of our first little house in Kabul; a gentleman was standing beside it.

"Why did your father have his picture taken there?" Julie asked.

"He likes the carpenter whose shop is next door to that house," Mina replied.

We told them we knew the carpenter because we had lived in that house.

Turning from the photo I heard Merwis say, "David, may I practice reading English with you?"

"Of course, Merwis," I answered.

From the bookshelf, he pulled out the paper I had written about the life of Christ and the difficulties He faced that were similar to those the refugees were facing. It was entitled, "The Unique Refugee."

Merwis was reading quite well. Only occasionally did I need to correct him. Suddenly, without warning, he impulsively and violently slapped the paper down on the couch.

"David, nobody, nobody, can be that good," he exclaimed, strongly accenting the final "nobody" by once again whacking the couch where he had left the paper.

Then he turned to me, his eyes flashing.

"You are right," I responded without raising my voice. "Nobody could be that good except God himself."

Merwis protested, "David, Christ is not God. He was a man, a prophet."

I knew his forceful defense to protect the honor of God was out of a sincere conscience, and I admired the honesty that motivated his protest.

"But, Merwis," I said, "isn't God great and almighty? Isn't He all-powerful?"

"Yes, He is" Merwis responded.

"Well, then didn't God have the power to come to the earth as a man in flesh and blood if He wanted to?" I asked.

Merwis' face looked very serious as I continued. "Merwis, I believe God did just that in Jesus. We cannot reach up to God, but He can reach down to us. He did so in the person of Jesus so we could know what God is like."

By now, Julie and Mina had joined our conversation as listeners.

"Merwis, you lived near me in Afghanistan and knew about me, but you did not know me. Now you and I have met personally and you know me. That is how it is with God. There is a difference between knowing about God and knowing God," I explained.

The conversation gradually drifted in other directions and finally we prepared to leave. Merwis and Mina walked us outside where we thanked them for their hospitality.

"It is nothing. Go in peace," they replied.

When we were free to talk alone, Julie said, "It was good that Merwis felt secure enough in his friendship with you to express himself about 'The Unique Refugee,' even if he was so forceful."

"Yes, it was. I really appreciate him," I responded.

Then she said, "David, what is the first thing you thought when you saw that photograph?"

"We're definitely going to Kabul!" I exclaimed.

"Right," she piped cheerily. "That's the first thing that came into my mind as well."

Several times I pondered my conversation with Merwis. When we saw each other briefly two days later, he seemed troubled.

Searching for the right words, Merwis said, "David, please be careful how you share what you believe with some people in some places."

Then, very quietly, he said, "Don't be so open. They won't understand."

"Thanks, Merwis. Thanks for caring. I promise to use wisdom," I replied sincerely.

As I drove home, the deepest part of me cried out to God, "Oh, Savior, why? Why is it so difficult for my friend Merwis and others like him to understand about You?"

To this day, that question has never been fully answered.

The day of our departure finally arrived. We had our suitcases packed, tickets to New Delhi in hand, and passports in order. The only thing unprepared was my heart. I was unprepared to say good-bye to these lovely and understanding people whom we had learned to love.

To have to leave them was hard enough, but to simultaneously receive the news most of them had just been denied permission to go to the United States was devastating. Their long preparations seemed in vain. The news crushed their dreams, and now we, their friends, were leaving Frankfurt.

My prayer to heaven that night was a question. "God, what am I going to say to them tomorrow at the airport?"

God's message to me was that I was not to worry about speaking to them or about having any special words. *Tomorrow your life will speak*, He seemed to say.

We arrived at the airport early, yet some of our Afghan friends were already there. Others gradually arrived, quiet and subdued. Tears were just one blink away from their soft dark eyes.

When we walked from the main lobby down the long concourse to the passport area—the last place visitors can accompany passengers—they walked with us. They refused to walk in front or beside us; rather they walked behind us, for we were their teachers. The manners of our former students, many of whom were professionals, humbled us beyond description.

Only one older man, Mr. Rashide, walked along beside us, talking as we walked.

"Why do you have to go now, David? Do you have to go? David, now who's going to tell us we're going to make it?" His questions tumbled out rapidly, giving me no time to respond in between.

In a final gesture of affection, the Afghans made a semicircle around us. Julie hugged each woman and I each man. Then we said a few words of thanks.

As we turned to go through the final door to the lounge for passengers only, Mr. Rashide's words echoed in my mind, *David, now who's going to tell us we're going to make it?*

The unanswered question hung in the air.

We paused in the doorway fighting tears, then turned and slowly walked out of their sight.

The couch in the passengers' lounge received us like a mother takes her child. We buried our faces in our hands and wept unashamedly, oblivious to those around us who had no idea of the depth of our sorrow or our sense of loss. We were torn between helping our dear friends in Frankfurt and obeying God's bidding.

When it was time, we got quietly to our feet to walk to our plane. Though I could no longer see them, I turned toward the direction I knew they would be, and from my heart whispered, "Good-bye, my friends, good-bye."

18

INCREDIBLE CERTAINTY

As the Pan Am DC-10 lifted into the leaden skies over Frankfurt, Julie and I sat near the back of the giant plane, too heartbroken to even look out the window. Our friends didn't even know we were headed for their beloved Afghanistan, for I was not free to tell them. Although I had direction from God about going to Afghanistan, I certainly had no visa from the government.

As I agonized over our loss, I suddenly felt the forceful presence of the Lord.

David, I know how heartbreaking this is for you. I know you did this out of obedience to Me and I am pleased. Be assured you are going back to Kabul. When you are able to tell this to your Afghan friends you have left behind, it will help them understand. I love them even more than you do.

A few hours later the pilot announced we were approaching the beautiful city of New Delhi, India. After landing and clearing customs, airport porters swarmed around us like bees and grabbed at our bags as we stepped out the main door. All of them shouted for attention as they jostled each other, reaching for our suitcases. Having experienced such encounters before, I simply but firmly pointed to two men to carry our luggage and declined speaking to the others.

Meanwhile taxi drivers called to me. "Good price, Mister!

This way. This way!"

I selected one and asked him if his meter worked. He assured me it did and I assured him I would not pay him if it did not. We knowingly grinned at each other. The luggage was piled on top of the little four-cylinder black cab and tied down. The perspiring driver put his arm out the window to ward off other cars and we lurched into the traffic flow, the meter clicking.

Not an easy life, I thought.

We arrived at an inexpensive hotel and checked in.

That week I arranged to meet with Bill Thompson, the director of the international medical team in Kabul I had contacted. Bill had recently arrived in New Delhi from Afghanistan. I was anxious to find out about my visa application. My heart raced as we rode in a rickshaw to the hotel near downtown New Delhi to meet him.

Bill had white hair and a fuzzy beard. In his early sixties, he was full of faith and didn't hesitate to take a risk if he felt he should.

"Well, Bill, what has the government said about my application?" I asked. We were sitting on the grass next to the hotel.

"Dave," he said, growing serious, "I'm sorry but they won't permit us to submit an application for you."

"But, Bill, I thought from the telegram you sent that an application was accepted. Are you saying that no application is in?"

"That's right," Bill replied. "I meant that we were again asking unofficially and were waiting for a reply."

I wondered how I had misunderstood his telegram. I had come to New Delhi believing I had an application in process.

"Will you please do me a big favor?" I asked.

"What's that?"

"Will you please go back to Kabul and ask the communist government once again if you can put an application in for me to teach English?" I knew my request was unreasonable and that he had already made this request two times, but I also knew God had spoken to me in Frankfurt about returning to Kabul. "I know it will take a big miracle," I admitted. "But we believe in miracles."

He thought for a moment then replied, "I'll do it. But I can't promise anything."

"Thanks. And please politely lean on the government for a reply. I can't stay in India forever. This is now the middle of March and I need to know by the 24th of April if the government will accept an application for me. Julie and I haven't been able to take a vacation for two years, so we're going to south India on the Arabian Sea to rest. At the end of that time, I need an answer if at all possible."

Bill nodded.

"There is one other thing I should mention," I concluded. "I have an Indian friend named Joseph whom God has spoken to about Kabul. I want to help him get a visa. Could I bring him by tomorrow?"

"Sure," Bill replied, "I'll be glad to talk with him."

Bill met Joseph and was impressed with his sincerity.

"I'll do what I can to get all of you to Kabul," he told us. That's all we needed to hear.

A few days later, Joseph, Julie, and I shoved our luggage into place and sat down on the wooden seats of the train to Trivandrum, Kerala, South India. The train jerked forward with its whistle blowing. We had begun our 60-hour, second-class journey to the Arabian Sea. About 1,500 people were on board for the 1,800-mile trip.

This is the way to see India, I thought. Mile after scenic mile rolled by. I especially felt at ease since Joseph, who lived in Kerala, was with us.

Countless stops, bag lunches, and fitful catnaps later, we arrived at Trivandrum. Joseph went to his home and we hired a taxi to look for a place to stay. Before long we were able to rent a small cottage near the ocean.

Out the window of our cabin, scarcely a hundred yards from the Indian Ocean, we watched the magnificent waves rhythmically wash the beach. In the evenings, Julie and I sat high on the rocks and watched the sun rest on the water like a giant floating balloon before it slowly sank from view. It was almost impossible not to relax and be refreshed.

In the mornings, we watched fishermen dive from their carved-out, ancient-looking boats into the depths of the sea and stay under for unbelievable periods of time. Occasionally, several boats would use one big circular net to catch fish.

Near the end of our vacation time, we felt renewed and eager to get to Kabul. We had begun to wonder why we had not heard from Bill when an aerogramme arrived from his associate in Kabul. Julie and I decided to open it at our favorite place on the high rocks over the sea.

I opened it carefully, unfolded the blue paper, and read:

"Dear Dave and Julie, We are so sorry to have to tell you that the government will not accept an application for you. There is nothing else we can do. This is the third time we have asked. We cannot ask again. I'm sure you understand. It will take the kind of miracle you talked about in order to obtain a visa. We are praying for you. Your friend in Kabul, Edwin."

I was surprised at my own response. Instead of feeling depressed or discouraged, I felt a mysterious sense of assurance and encouragement.

"Julie, you know something?" I asked. " I know we are going to Kabul."

Julie smiled and laughed easily, "Yes, I know we are. But it's going to be interesting to see how God arranges it."

Two days later, while we were sitting in a restaurant, a messenger handed a telegram to me. It read: "Julie urgently needed to fill a position on the medical team. May we put in an application? Please reply immediately. Signed, Bill, Kabul, Afghanistan."

"Well, honey, what do you think of that?" I asked Julie, who was still sorting out her emotions. Then teasingly I continued, "I hope I can go with you. The telegram doesn't say a word about me."

She grinned and said she would try to arrange it.

We were glad Joseph and his wife, Sarah, were coming to see us the next day so we could share the good news. We prayed that night, offering thanksgiving for the sudden miracle. But then we felt it was only right to ask Joseph, who was more qualified, to take the position Julie was being offered. We would not telegram Kabul until we spoke with him.

Sitting together with Joseph and Sarah and their two young children, we told them about the telegram.

"Joseph, we think you should apply for this position. You are more qualified. We'll find another way."

"Thank you both," Joseph responded. "That's very thoughtful of you but God has definitely opened the door for you. Julie is the one who should apply for the position, not me."

"Are you sure, Joseph?"

"I'm sure, Dave. Once you're in Kabul it will be easier to find a way for me to get a visa. Then we'll join you."

"Okay, if you think that's best."

Something wonderful and good took place between God's servants on that rock by the sea. The four of us and the children prayed together. We talked about how we believed the day would come when we would have tea together in Kabul. I was determined to find a way for Joseph and Sarah to obtain visas for Afghanistan.

We wired Bill to submit an application for Julie. Expecting the normal two- to three-month wait for a reply from the government, we prepared to enjoy what we hoped would be our final weeks in India. At Kodai Kanal, a hill station in southern India, we found a little cabin with very reasonable rent where we spent our time praying and catching up on correspondence.

To our surprise, 30 days after Julie's application had been submitted, she was approved for a visa and I was able to obtain my visa as her dependent spouse.

We packed our bags, flew to New Delhi, and went straight to the Afghan Embassy. A cold, bureaucratic-looking clerk informed us an official wanted to see us. Without a doubt, the clerk had the power to stamp our entry visas because he showed me the telegrammed order from Kabul. Perhaps the higher official wanted to see us in person because it was extremely rare for Americans to be granted entry visas for Afghanistan.

After a guide was called, he led us upstairs and down a hallway to a large door. He knocked and a suave-looking Afghan with a cigarette in his hand opened the door. The man greeted us warmly and introduced himself as Comrade Farid. Something about him struck me as too slick, too polite.

My heart suddenly started pounding as the smooth-talking man introduced us to three other men in the room whom he called comrades. Nervously, I shook hands with each one and was then directed to sit on a plush couch.

Feeling intimidated, I asked God to calm my heart and turn the tables.

Behind an imposing desk, Farid, who looked to be in his early thirties, smiled nervously. "We should not allow the differences between our governments to interfere with performing humanitarian duties," he said. I nodded my head slightly but said nothing.

"I would like to tell you about Kabul," he continued.

"Fine," I said.

He and the others went into a long detailed description about the weather in Kabul.

"Of course you have never been to Kabul," stated Farid.

"Yes, we have lived in Kabul before," I replied.

The four comrades looked at each other in surprise. Then there followed an embarrassing moment of silence.

With an uncomfortable smile, Farid finally said, "Well, we hope you have an enjoyable time in Kabul. Good changes are taking place."

"Thank you," I said.

Julie and I were politely dismissed. After we were handed our passports with those beautiful new entry visas, we rode away from the Embassy in a cab. However, I couldn't get the seemingly trapped man behind the desk off my mind, and I wondered about his future.

Three days later, which was as fast as we could make arrangements and get tickets, we flew to Kabul. No two happier people ever walked through that city's airport.

About three months later, God made it possible for Joseph, Sarah, and their two children to join us in Kabul. We all knew the Lord was in control. And it was a good thing too, for tense, mysterious, and dangerous times were approaching.

19

WHO RANG THE DOORBELL?

Arriving in Kabul, I yearned to see our trusted teacher, Mr. Munsif, and our former language helper, Ajmal. They were not aware the impossible had taken place and we were back in their city. I knew it would be dangerous to meet with them, but I asked God to make that possible and to protect us.

To my great consternation, I discovered Mr. Munsif and his family had moved. I didn't know where to find him, and to ask would possibly net me more trouble than good information. I walked the streets constantly, looking for his familiar face or the face of one of his family. With all the crowded streets it seemed futile, but I kept petitioning God for help.

It was six months before a mutual friend risked giving me the address of a shop where Mr. Munsif received his mail. On my behalf, another friend wrote a note for me and delivered it to the shop. Arrangements were made for Mr. Munsif to meet me privately in a public office building two days after he received my message. Hopefully, by meeting in a public place, suspicion would not be aroused.

Irritation about the whole idea plagued my thoughts. *What troubled times dictated such caution just for friends to spend time together. Why can't we just meet freely as families and companions?*

I reached the office a few minutes before Mr. Munsif and sat in the room silently thanking God I had, at least, found my teacher. When I looked out the window and saw Mr. Munsif slowly approaching the building, I grappled for control of the strong emotions welling up inside.

My teacher greeted me with a strong embrace. He later told me he had not slept the two nights after receiving my message. Our hour together flew by too swiftly, and as my friend walked away I was already sketching ways in my mind to see him and his family more often.

Although Ajmal and his family were much easier to contact, only twice during the next 13 months did we take the high risk of meeting them. Both were memorable family reunions with much laughter and prayer. Still, a pall hung over us because we knew the house could be searched by soldiers at any time and Julie's and my presence meant possible arrest for all of us. In spite of the danger, we rejoiced together, believing God would guard the house.

Feeling God's protection in this war-torn nation was no license to be foolish, but I did feel free to enter old bazaars where Russians wouldn't go for fear of being killed or kidnapped. People would ask, sometimes incredulously, where I was from and I would answer, "America." I'd hear them say to one another in Pushtu or Dari, "No, he's not an American. He's just a Russian who speaks English well," or "He's not telling the truth; he just wants us to like him." Once in a while, if the situation warranted, I'd show my passport. For the most part, however, it was hopeless. They could not conceive of an American in their midst.

One day, I meandered down the muddy street in the market area, stopping for a moment to speak briefly with shopkeepers. None would talk with me very long, which was understandable considering the circumstances.

At one point a Pushtun shopkeeper, maybe 30 years of age, asked me where I was from and I told him. Pushtuns are usually very up-front people and he was no exception. Fearlessly, he had me sit down to tea and told me he had a brother in West Germany. Information about the whereabouts of relatives was not usually shared, yet he seemed unworried.

A short time later an Afghan wearing a sport coat over traditional clothing approached us. He said to the shopkeeper, "Who is this guy?" He didn't know I could understand his Pushtu. I saw a gun under his coat.

The shopkeeper's response was, "Oh, he's just an American sitting here."

The man with the gun looked at me and laughed out loud.

After he left, the Pushtun shopkeeper laughed even harder. He hadn't known what to say to the gun-toting stranger, so he told the absolute truth—truth so preposterous the man didn't believe it.

It was the same with Afghan soldiers. They would often laugh before asking me, "Where are you really from?"

One night while lying on my bed my mind went back a few months to March 1982—just before we left Germany. A good friend Nathan Barnes and his wife were helping us prepare to leave. It was after midnight when we finally got everything ready and they were about to go home.

As Nathan approached our door, he felt prompted by the Spirit of God to say, "David and Julie, I feel I have a word from the Lord to share. 'As the mountains surround

Kabul, so I, the Lord, will surround you. For anyone to touch you they must come over Me.'"

This prophetic word convinced us no harm would come. However, if something did happen, it would make no difference to us, for God was with us. Whether we were protected or persecuted, whether we lived or died, whether we were arrested or free, we had peace—peace so strong it could not be dissipated or destroyed.

Danger was our daily companion. Using a balance of trust and wisdom, I freely moved about. The dangers in Afghanistan were very real for everyone. Sometimes the night would snatch innocent people from their homes and the morning acted as if they never existed.

Ten o'clock curfew was again in effect. Rarely did any but the bravest soul venture out after sundown. I recalled the words my mom had spoken before we left the United States: "The safest place in the world is in the will of God. You are safer in Afghanistan in His will than in the United States if you're out of His will."

One particular evening we returned to our house well before dark, ate our meal, and read for a while before retiring for the night.

As I turned off the kerosene lamps, Julie called to me from the bedroom, "David, look at the snow!" Once in bed, we snuggled down deep into the soft cotton quilts to avoid the chilled air. By 10 o'clock we were sound asleep.

Shortly after midnight, a single doorbell ring startled us out of our dreams. Immediately we were fully alert. We knew only the military or secret police were likely visitors after curfew. Holding my breath while we waited for the dreaded second ring, I could see a look of alarm on Julie's face.

Thoughts raced through my mind: *That's it; they've come for me. It's all over. What will they say? What reasons will be made? Will any excuses be given? Innocence is no defense.*

"Lord, help Julie," I prayed softly, feeling a sharp pang of sorrow for her.

The ponderous silence was broken only by the pounding of my own heart. On impulse I sat up. *But wait. See if they ring again. If they do, I'll go to the door before they break in.*

Be ready, I thought. *It's all right, God, I'm in Your hands.*

Minutes passed slowly as we waited in the dark without speaking. But nothing happened. There was no second ring. We lay down once again, but could not go back to sleep.

"Maybe it was a mistake." Julie whispered. I could detect the tremor in her forced whisper.

"Maybe so," I answered, trying to sound calm.

The morning light revealed fresh footprints in the snow. The long exposed doorbell wire to the house from the gate was frayed in places. Did the snow short it out? If so, why only one long ring? Then we saw the red drops on the pure white snow.

Oh, no! Did someone need help? I thought. *What did it mean?*

I did not know. The black night never gave a reason for being so dark, and the silent, snowy footprint never whispered an excuse for being stained.

Throughout Afghanistan a sense of instability prevailed. People were nervous about the changes in their land. They had seen a coup and a Soviet invasion, and they knew their security was threatened.

Afghan families were cautious about asking any foreigners into their homes. Even when we received an invitation, we tried to discern if the Lord wanted us to accept. We did not want to do anything that would unnecessarily jeopardize the lives of our friends. When we would go, the family would leave its front gate unlocked rather than come out to greet us as they would have in normal times.

Responding to an invitation from our first landlord, Dr. Shafe, Julie and I left our house one November night to walk to his home. We were usually a little skittish when we walked because we knew my blond hair, light complexion, and blue eyes made me look Russian. There was a tongue-in-cheek rumor that no Afghan government troops were disloyal and that they would never shoot Russians. However, the night before there had been a shootout in our neighborhood and no one knew who shot whom or why.

After our visit with the Shafes, we walked toward our home as quickly as possible. Though we were afraid we would arouse suspicion if we walked too quickly, we still felt a sense of urgency to get off the street as soon as possible. At the street corner, where the high walls met, we ran straight into a night patrol—eight Afghan soldiers slowly walking two abreast about 10 feet apart. Their startled look matched ours. I recovered and offered greetings to them in Pushtu. Two returned the greetings.

I wished my accent wasn't so noticeable.

To get to our house, we had to turn right and go down the same street as the soldiers. As we made the turn we found ourselves walking between two sets of soldiers.

My mind began to race. Shall we continue this slow pace or go ahead of them? What do they think about our being on the street? Will they take special note of where we live? What about that "troop loyalty" rumor? If shooting breaks out, will we be caught in the crossfire?

I quickly breathed a prayer and, taking Julie's arm, opted to go ahead of them.

After a few steps I heard a giggle. Julie's thoughts had turned to a highly respected friend of ours, Charles Greenaway. This man spent many years overseas, and he often said inspiring things about the difficulties he faced and how he triumphed over many situations. His positive philosophy was wrapped up in these words: "If you're about to get run out of town, get in front and make it look like you're leading a parade."

Because of the potentially dangerous situation, I was about to hush Julie when she whispered, "Charles would be proud of us, David. We're leading the parade."

When we got in our house, our crazy, mixed-up feelings were released as we burst into laughter. Then we thanked God for safety.

From time to time, I'd visit my friend Syed at his electrical workshop. Our chats were always enjoyable.

I remember the first time I saw him upon my return to Afghanistan in 1982. This was my third stay in the capital, and he knew that most Western foreigners had left Afghanistan.

Syed was overjoyed to see me, yet in disbelief and with a great deal of alarm in his voice he exclaimed, "David, what are you doing here? It's dangerous for you. People are trying to escape and you return of your own accord." His deep-set eyes registered his concern as he repeated, "What are you doing here?"

"Syed," I said, "I'm here because I love God,

Afghanistan, and you, my friend."

It was hard for people to understand why we continued to stay in such a situation. That we were motivated by love seemed unbelievable. If we were political or had come to Afghanistan for financial gain, that was understandable, even though the circumstances were so dangerous. However, few seemed to grasp that a God-given love for people was motivation enough for Julie and me to remain.

However, even during this time of turmoil and fear among the people, I made friends in Afghanistan. And none were more appreciative of our kindness than a special group of men who helped me do warehouse work and deliver medical supplies.

20

MY LIKABLE, UNLETTERED FRIENDS

In the spring of 1983 I felt the need for more in-depth prayer. A deeper communion with God prompted me to set aside two hours a day for this purpose. I also felt I needed to find a place to pray that was apart from our home.

Behind our house was a tall, empty office building badly in need of repair. Plans were to convert the building into a two-family dwelling, and though this renovation had begun the owners gave me permission to use the building each morning from 5:30 to 7:30.

"My" room on the second floor was empty except for a straight-backed chair and a lone lightbulb. Fortunately, a window afforded light and a nice view of Kabul. No workers came until later in the day.

After reading several chapters from my Bible, I would pray. Sometimes I would kneel, but most often I paced back and forth across the room. My prayer life was being revolutionized by this time of unhurried, uninterrupted praise and petition. The two hours passed swiftly, and my anticipation of this time alone with God was fresh each morning. I felt really free during this time of prayer—unlike the rest of my severely restricted situation—experiencing marvelous times of fellowship with God.

I enjoyed worshipping in the Spirit and praying for the people of Afghanistan in my native tongue and unknown tongue. Sometimes I sang in English, and occasionally I would even sing in Pushtu. As I prayed, I wondered how to make the Afghan people aware of God's love. I felt limited and inadequate for the task. Every day I agonized for Kabul, the nation of Afghanistan, and the Pushtun people.

A *chawkidar* (night watchman) kept guard over the unsupervised building where I prayed. This man was in his mid-twenties. Normally at that age he would have been in the army, but a severe physical disability kept him out of the service.

His face always needed shaving, but I never minded because of his ready smile. He was very thin and looked malnourished, but he worked hard. He genuinely wanted to help, and he was always hurrying to do small kindnesses. I learned the man was trying to support his family who had been bombed out of one of the villages. I doubt he owned more than one change of clothes.

This *chawkidar* lived in a small, sparsely furnished room that contained a cot covered by a worn cotton quilt and an electric hot plate that sat on the floor beside a bowl and two cups. The only color relief from the dingy gray walls was a picture of a flower that hung next to a screened window that had a hole in it.

Not only did the *chawkidar* watch the building, but he also kept an eye on my car when I parked there. It bothered me that I could hardly communicate with him, for I spoke very little of his Dari language.

Since he was responsible for security, I always let him know when I was about to enter the building. I wanted him to be aware I was there. Often I'd tell him I was going upstairs to pray. Whether he understood what I was doing, I didn't know. But each day I would mention the *chawkidar* to God as I prayed.

Later, after a family moved into the building, the *chawkidar* told a friend of mine, "You know, all the time Mr. Daoud prayed in that room I would sit on the step under the window and listen and often cry."

I never knew he was there, nor that he wept with me. But he told my friend that those times made him feel good. I felt humbled and happy when I heard this.

Was God's love somehow revealed to him? What other things were hidden in the unseen power of prayer?

The *chawkidar* had a difficult life for he was also a day laborer. Such workers are usually very poor and illiterate. Often they are men who are past their prime. They take the low-paying, backbreaking work no one else wants.

Five of them, including the *chawkidar*, were on the crew I supervised. Together we worked in a warehouse handling hospital equipment and medical supplies. My crew consisted of a plump, middle-aged driver and four workers. Only one of these men was less than 50 years of age.

All of them had leathery, deeply-lined faces. Three had full beards, and two had front teeth missing. Four of the men spoke Dari and one spoke Pushtu. Abdullah, who spoke both, acted as my translator from Pushtu to Dari. For the most part, they wore tattered, ill-fitting clothes and thin sandals that had been repaired often. Their outfits were topped off with either a turban or skullcap. Their loose-fitting clothes and ready smiles gave them a comical look, but their calloused hands and feet reminded me how difficult their lives were. Their enigmatic, ragged, simple appearance captivated me.

Three of them had arrived in Kabul with their large families from bombed-out villages. Two others were in the same straits, but they came from the city. All of them had pathetically few possessions and little money, but they were eager to work. To a Western observer we must have appeared to be a strange group as we loaded, unloaded, and transported boxes with our brown Toyota truck.

These illiterate men never had a chance to learn some of life's most basic skills, yet their warmth and humor endeared them to me. I had never before worked directly with the poor and illiterate, so I learned much from them. My friends and fellow-laborers were unknown to the world, and to most it did not matter if they existed. But they were important to God and I treated them that way.

The men served as night watchmen for various buildings and homes. Those jobs required their presence every night, all night long. Sometimes I would pedal my bike to where each one passed his lonely vigil. When I arrived and rang the bell, he would invite me into a little barren room, separate from the main building. I would sit with him for a while to chat and sip tea, hoping somehow he would know I cared. With the Dari speakers, verbal communication was next to impossible, yet I would visit each one for a while anyway.

Big, strong Habib was the natural leader of the crew. He actually knew more about the whole business than their inexperienced supervisor. His pleasant manner belied his tough look. I quickly realized the best way to get things done was to ask him what he thought, then let him review the situation and give me his opinion.

"That sounds fine with me," I'd say. "Please explain it to the others."

I tried to walk in their sandals and, to their surprise, labored alongside them in the heat of the day. My behavior perplexed them because I was in charge and didn't have to do such things. What astounded them most, perhaps, was when I rode in the back of the truck so one of them could take my place in the cab. We laughed together, though I suspected the joke often was on me. I didn't mind.

One summer day after finishing up a big load, I climbed on top of the truck to help two of the men tie the load down. Our labor in the afternoon heat was interrupted by the roar of a black Mercedes Benz on the dusty street nearby. A glance convinced me the car was traveling way too fast.

In the next instant, the sound of screeching tires and a loud thump brought a sickening sensation to my stomach. Then I heard the car start up again and speed away.

I could not see around the walled street corner to know what had happened, so I scrambled off the truck and dashed to the area. A boy on a bicycle had been hit and thrown against the wall. He was unconscious and bleeding. Shortly after I arrived at the scene, dozens of people appeared, shouting and jostling for a view. Upon seeing the boy's battered body, I felt the color drain from my face and my stomach tighten. Someone managed to stop a taxi and the boy was placed in the backseat, hopefully, for a trip to a hospital.

Another tragedy in Kabul, I thought. *Hasn't the war brought enough suffering to every family?*

Hit-and-run accidents like this only intensified my feelings of sorrow for the people of the city.

Would there be no end to their pain and grief? I was deeply saddened by their plight.

Slowly the laborers and I walked back to the truck. Feelings of hopelessness and utter helplessness robbed me of strength.

Then an idea began to come to me. "Please tell the men

to sit on the grass," I said to Abdullah. I proceeded very carefully because I did not want to offend my Muslim friends, whom I respected, yet I felt a strong urge to pray to Christ.

Abdullah translated as I said with boldness, "We are going to pray for the injured boy and his family."

The men, whose desperate lives left scant room or time for compassion outside their own families, just stared at me. I stretched out my hands in front of me, palms up in the Islamic prayer sign of submission. They quickly followed suit.

Although Muslims do not pray with their eyes closed, I did. A spontaneous prayer from my heart, spoken aloud in the name of my Savior, was uttered. As a few tears slipped down my face, I remembered that Afghan men seldom if ever cry, but I could not help it. For a few moments we remained silent.

Slowly, not knowing what to expect, I opened my eyes and looked into the motionless, solemn faces of the men whose eyes were red and moist.

For a few seconds I sat there, looking from countenance to countenance. In the brief moment I shared with each one as I turned my gaze toward him, something of tremendous value was silently communicated between us. I felt an extreme closeness with them. We were no longer East or West, boss or laborer. We were friends who had felt a boy's pain and God's presence. We had found refuge together in a harsh world.

All too quickly the time was once again approaching when Julie and I would have to return to the United States for a visit. Already it had been four years since we had seen our families.

Two nights before we left Afghanistan, I bicycled to each *chawkidar's* residence for the last time to say farewell. I sipped tea with each one, then I did what was always the most difficult thing for me to do in serving overseas: I said good-bye. Before I left his residence, I asked each friend if I could have the privilege of praying with him. Each one kindly agreed.

Whether it was culturally acceptable, I didn't really know, but I would put a hand on his shoulder as I sat on the edge of the cot and prayed aloud for his family and his future. Then, after the traditional three hugs, I would slip into the night. Pushing my bike several steps, I would turn back toward the place I had just left. Without exception I would see a solemn figure watching after me, framed in the light of the open door.

As Julie and I prepared to return to the United States, our pain of departure was eased because we knew we would return to Afghanistan. We also knew we had done our best to share Christ's love.

Awaiting us in America were not only our own loved ones, but also many Afghan friends. Soon after Julie and I had left our Afghan students in West Germany, the U.S. government had reversed its decision and permitted them entry.

What I did not know when I left Afghanistan was that I would be able to renew my friendship with an outstanding young Afghan man. Nor was I aware this friend was about to make one of the greatest discoveries of his life, and I would once again peek behind the curtain of circumstance to see the secret work of God.

21

HE'S NOT PLAYING GAMES

Kabul, New Delhi, Frankfurt, New York, Cleveland. Finally, my home in Ohio. However, I didn't really feel at home until I tasted Mom's homemade noodles and traveled with Dad on the roads of Bristolville and Howland.

I asked Dad if the fish were biting in Mosquito Lake.

"Walleyes are hittin' some," he replied. And indeed they were. But unfortunately the day he and I went fishing, we caught only panfish and a carp.

"I'll get 'em another day," he said with confidence.

After several days of visiting with each of our parents, we began to anticipate seeing other friends and loved ones. Julie was eager to catch up with everyone, to shop, and to give the gifts we had brought from Afghanistan.

One day she said, "David, let's map our route to see Lucy and my brother in Florida and, of course, Noel and Joyce in South Carolina, and our many Afghan friends in California and Virginia and ..."

"Okay, okay!" I laughed, "but let's take it one step at a time."

Quite soon we began our travels across the United States. Because of people's great interest in Afghanistan, many doors of opportunity were opened. We traveled the country speaking in conferences, seminars, churches, schools, and colleges—gladly helping Americans understand the Afghan people.

It was now 1985. As I drove the monotonous California Interstate, the boredom gave me a chance to reflect on the events that had occurred during the past few years. Together, Julie and I had tried to be obedient to the Lord, no matter where His path for us had led.

I glanced over at Julie, my napping copilot, and thought, *What a beauty she is.*

It was a blessing being married to her—a unique gift from God and the answer to my prayer for a wife who loved God as much as I did. From Lansing, Illinois, to Kabul, Afghanistan, and all points between, Julie had believed in me and my impossible plans and she was just as eager as I to someday return to Afghanistan. I recalled her promise to me that no matter where I died she would be sure to have my body buried in Afghanistan. I knew she would keep that promise.

She knows my failures and frailties better than anyone but God, yet she loves me completely, I thought. Taking a deep breath, I smiled and thanked God once more for my wife.

Like shifting desert sands, thoughts of Afghan friends started filling my mind. If I had not obeyed the Lord, I would never have realized so many beautiful friendships—friendships I prayed would last forever. My life would have been so much poorer without trusted friends like Mr. Munsif or Ajmal.

Ahead I saw a sign marking the turnoff to Anwar's. I quickly scooted the car over two lanes and exited. As I neared my friend's house, I began thinking about him and about our friendship that had begun several years before.

Anwar was a teenager when we first met; now he was an articulate man in his early twenties. He was one who exhibited both shyness and self-confidence. What made him stand out most was his inquisitive mind. The everyone's-doing-it mentality didn't make sense to Anwar. He had to know and understand why. As we became better acquainted, I highly valued his friendship.

Beside me Julie stirred from her nap. With her flair for map reading, she soon steered us to Anwar's front door. We were greeted by only Anwar and his sister; we were told the rest of the family would join us later.

While we waited for the other family members to return home, Anwar and I took a leisurely stroll. At a nearby park we stopped alongside a weeping willow tree whose branches reached out over the lake like protecting arms.

"I like to come here to relax," Anwar said.

We sat on the grassy bank of the lake in the shade of the willow. I listened to him carefully as he mused about some of life's most puzzling questions. I was amazed at the clarity of his thinking and his insight.

Anwar paused as he tossed a small pebble into the water, then leaned back against the tree, his fingers laced behind his head. "Dave, I have concluded that knowing God must be the greatest thing in life," he said in a relaxed, convincing way.

I had not expected such a crystalline statement. It seemed to come straight from his heart as he looked at me with eyes full of resolve. The depth and purity of his words held me in silence. Finally, I asked, "Anwar, how did you reach that conclusion?"

He responded, "I have thought about life. What caused me to look hard at life was my stay in Pul-I-Charkhi prison."

By prison he was referring to the time when, as a youth, he had to spend a short time in jail for being in a student demonstration against the communists in Kabul.

He continued, "Until that time, I was a happy person. Things always seemed to go well for me. I was always a good person, trying hard to do what was right. But being locked up in prison caused me to start thinking about the meaning of life. I'm glad for my stay in prison. If it hadn't been for that, perhaps I never would have thought seriously about life."

He leaned forward and shifted his position before continuing.

"In recent months, I have looked inside myself. When I look within, I know that without God there is no hope. When I look at the world's situation and into the future, I see no hope without God. I have carefully observed this materialistic society where people have things but are not happy. They work hard but are constantly exhausted. They only exist and have a false sense of security because they seek pleasure that cannot last. Without God life is short and meaningless."

As Anwar spoke, I reflected on our conversations of more than a year before. He had taken an incredible journey of growth in his thinking since then. Eighteen months ago he had asked many sincere, yet skeptical questions, and I had tried my best to answer them.

I had told Anwar not to believe what I said just because I said it. I urged him to sincerely ask God to reveal truth to him. Right then and there he did so. I humbly listened as he spoke to God.

Anwar had so much to share with me. "Dave, this year I have read the works of a number of great thinkers in history. They ask the right questions but don't have the answers."

"How true," I responded as I thought about the endless hours I, too, had studied such men's writings.

"Knowing God has to be the greatest thing in life," Anwar repeated.

"Anwar, please tell me, how does one know God?"

Embarrassed, Anwar smiled, "You have me there. You really have me there."

"Anwar, we don't know God because our relationship with Him has been broken by sin. Christ's death on the cross restores that broken relationship when we repent of our sin and accept His forgiveness."

My friend listened closely.

"Anwar, the only One to ever walk on earth who was perfect was Christ. Have you ever struggled with sin in your own heart? Have you ever done wrong when you thought no one was looking?"

"I have struggled," he admitted. "I don't want to sin, but it troubles me when you say Christ died for us. That seems so unfair."

"You're right, Anwar, but He paid the price voluntarily. There was no other way for our sin to be forgiven. That happened because God loves us."

Anwar replied, "But why does God love us? God doesn't need us."

"That's correct, Anwar. He doesn't need anyone or anything. But it's God's very nature to love us."

Anwar looked quizzically at me.

"Anwar, do a husband and wife need a child in order to know what true love is?" I asked.

"No," he answered.

"But a husband and wife have children because they want to share their love, not because they need a child to experience love. God doesn't need us, Anwar, but He wants to share His love with us. Sin is what separates us from knowing God. Christ is the bridge. To know Him is to know God and experience His love."

The sun was setting and it had become chilly. We got up, brushed off our clothes, and started up the slope. Suddenly Anwar slapped me on the back and exclaimed, "That's it, Dave, that's it."

"What's it, Anwar?"

"That's the answer to the question I asked you over a year ago." His voice was full of excitement.

My mind scrambled to recall the question he had asked me.

"You know, Dave, I asked you if God was playing games with the human race because there is so much evil in the world, so much injustice. I thought perhaps He was. Now you have answered me."

Then I remembered what I'd told him. I'd said, "One reason evil and injustice are rampant in the world is because God has given men freedom of choice. Men have a will. We are not machines. Men abuse free choice and cause chaos in the world. Yet without free choice, there would be no love or loving people—only robots."

Puzzled, I said, "Excuse me, Anwar, how did I answer that question today?"

"Dave, God loves us. He really loves us. That's why He is not playing games."

Joyously, I patted Anwar on the back. He had discovered God was not a cold, calculating, impersonal force or being to whom we are enslaved. Rather, He is the infinite God who personally loves each person.

Now Anwar had felt that great love. Anwar's eyes twinkled as he basked serenely in that truth. He smiled broadly.

It was quiet as we walked back to the house. As I took each step, Anwar's words echoed in my mind, *Dave, God loves us. He's not playing games.*

Oh, God, how many others are there who struggle to understand and receive Your love, but there is no one to tell them how?

Thank you, God, for not playing games with me.

Thank you for allowing me to experience Your love over and over each day.

And dear God, thank You for allowing me to share Your love with the people for whom You have given me immeasurable love.

"How often I have longed to gather your children together, as a hen gathers her chicks under her wings" (Matthew 23:37).

Lord, You have placed this verse in my heart. As You wept over Jerusalem, so do I weep over Afghanistan and its people who have been scattered to the far corners of the earth. Tears of sorrow do I weep, because their house too has been left desolate.

Afghanistan, my tears flow and my prayers rise for you.

Afghanistan ... my tears.

Since the conclusion of this book, David and Julie Leatherberry have continued to serve the Afghans.

They worked with the international relief organization Shelter Now for more than two years in Pakistan, where David served as the director of a milk program for Afghan refugee children. Forty-four wonderful Afghan refugee men worked with him to give more than 19,000 children each a liter of milk five days a week.

Julie and her German coworker Irmgard were invited by the government of Pakistan and the United Nations to develop a community and training center for Afghan war widows. In a culturally sensitive way, they diligently established this, bringing hope and happiness to the widows. Because the fanatics could not tolerate the success of the center or the love that was shown at this facility, they caused a riot and the center was destroyed.

In the summer of 1991, David and Julie were requested to go to northern Iraq for two months to lead a small team to establish a relief project for the Kurdish people. While there, they lived in a small tent next to a destroyed village. The project was established and within two years, more than 6,000 shelters were constructed for the Kurds.

After their short stay in Iraq, David and Julie returned to Pakistan to continue assisting Afghans through relief efforts.

From 1993-1997, the Leatherberrys were based in Central/Eastern Europe where they assisted displaced Afghans. David was also a guest lecturer at colleges in this area of the world.

Near the end of 1997 through 1999, the couple lived in Kandahar, Afghanistan, under the rule of the Taliban, five blocks from the Taliban leader Mullah Omar. David served as director of a small pre-cast roofing beam factory for Shelter Now.

Based in Cyprus during 2000-2003, the Leatherberrys traveled to different countries of the former Soviet Union, where David was a guest lecturer at colleges.

In 2003, David and Julie moved to Yekaterinburg, Russia, where they presently reside. They have founded the national newspaper *Afghanets*, a specialized publication for the former Soviet soldiers who are veterans of the Soviet/Afghan War. There are more than 1,000,000 of such veterans, thousands of whom were traumatized as young men by the war. David and Julie have been warmly received by these men because of the couple's experience in Afghanistan during the war.

The Leatherberrys dream of returning someday to Afghanistan with veterans from the former Soviet Union whose lives have been changed by Christ to help bring reconciliation between them and the former Afghan warriors.

David has a great desire to be buried in Afghanistan because of his love for Afghans. These are the people he wants to be among when the Great Resurrection Day occurs!